OUR BIBLE

I

HOW WE GOT IT

By Rev. Charles Leach, D.D.

II

TEN REASONS WHY I BELIEVE THE BIBLE IS THE WORD OF GOD

By R. A. Torrey

MOODY PRESS

PREFACE.

HAVE written this book for my own pleasure and profit; and now publish it, hoping to give pleasure and profit to others.

In its preparation I have made use of such material as I thought suitable, wherever I found it, and I desire to acknowledge most fully my indebtedness to a large number of able writers whose works I have been able to consult. Among them I desire to mention Dr. Westcott, Dr. R. W. Dale, Dr. Newth, Dr. J. P. Smyth, Thomas Cooper, Dr. Tischendorf, "Smith's Bible Dictionary," and many others.

Should any of the multitude of busy people who love the Bible obtain help from the following pages, no one will rejoice more than the busy man who has written them.

CHARLES LEACH.

Manchester, 189?.

CONTENTS.

PART I. —THE NEW TESTAMENT.

PART II. —THE OLD TESTAMENT.

PART III. —OUR ENGLISH BIBLE.

Is My Bible True?

Where did we get it?

PART I.—THE NEW TESTAMENT.

I.

INTRODUCTION.

 ONCE said to a Christian lady, "Is the Bible really true?" Without a moment's hesitation she answered, "Of course it is true." But when I asked her how she would proceed to *prove* it to be true, she could not answer me. *Could you?*

If I were to ask you where the Bible came from, who wrote it, and when and where, you might not be able to tell me readily. And yet these questions can be answered by those who have had time to study the subjects which they raise.

There are thousands of people all over the world

who love the Bible as the best of all books. It is
their daily companion and friend. They accept it
as the inspired Word of God. They come to it for
comfort when they are sad, for guidance when per-
plexed, and for instruction in those matters of the
soul and God which they cannot obtain elsewhere.
It has quickened them into new life, and been to
them one of God's agents in kindling on the altar of
their hearts those flames of immortal glory which
reach beyond the bounds of time. It inspires many
of them to deeds of love and sacrifice, which make
the world richer and better. The poor among them
read it, and learn to sing songs of joy and gladness
in their poverty. The rich among them read it,
and many of them discover that they are stewards
for God, and that the gold and silver which they hold
belong to Him. The tempted and the tried find it
a source of new strength and hope.

THE MASSES LOVE THE BIBLE.

Among these people are many of the excellent
of the earth. Thousands of them would suffer any
loss rather than part with the Bible. In the first
centuries of the Christian era many were cast into
prison rather than give up their Scriptures to those
who were engaged upon the impossible task of exter-
minating the Bible. Numbers of them suffered death
itself rather than dishono: the Word of the living

God. Among the masses of the people to-day there are multitudes who have the same loyal love for the inspired Book, and if occasion demanded it, would endure death rather than dishonor it.

And yet many of them could not answer my questions. It is to help such as these that I write these pages. I want them to know that the Bible which we have is substantially the same as that possessed by our Lord and His Apostles and the Christians in the first century.

There is one thing of which we are all sure—*the Bible is here.* Wherever it came from, whoever made it—we possess it. True or false, good or bad, of men or of God, inspired or uninspired, it is among us.

Our fathers had it before us. *Their* copies of the Scriptures are in our possession, not a few of them marked and made precious with the tears they shed upon the pages, hallowed with the breath of their prayers. Their fathers had it, too. Where did they get it? In order to discover its truth, we will

TRACE IT BACK TO ITS SOURCE.

The River Thames flows through London. It bears on its bosom the ships of all nations, which carry the merchandise of the world. Below London it flows into the ocean, and puts the nation in touch with all parts of the globe. It is interesting to follow it backward, and see it as it flows through quiet

valleys, past ancient cities and many a mile of peaceful scenery. Londoners do not like their old river
any the less when they discover that it has its source
as a small stream among the distant hills, and grows
to be the noble river it is as it passes London after
many other rivers and streams have flowed into it.
In like manner, we shall love our Bible no less,
but more, when we know how it came into the world
and grew to be the noble book it is.

I shall have to take you on journeys to different
cities and distant lands. We shall have to visit
many libraries, examine old books and parchments,
consult ancient records, and peep into some churches
venerable with age. We shall have to visit ancient
monasteries, and sit beside some of the old monks
who are now safe in the better land.

We want to know, as far as we can learn, how
to answer the following questions:

I.   Is the Bible really true?

II.   Where did our Bible come from?

III.   Is our Bible the same which the ancient
Christians read daily?

IV.   Were the contents of our New Testament in
our hands, in the hands of the Apostles and their
friends and followers before the first century had
closed?

V.—Is the Old Testament which we peruse the
same which our Lord had?

We shall deal first with the New Testament, and then with the Old, and then we shall trace the history of our English Bible. May the spirit of God who inspired the holy Apostles help us and guide us in the way of all truth!

II.

CHRIST BEFORE THE GOSPELS.

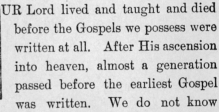UR Lord lived and taught and died before the Gospels we possess were written at all. After His ascension into heaven, almost a generation passed before the earliest Gospel was written. We do not know that He wrote a line, except with His finger on the floor of the Temple when the Pharisees brought a fallen woman into his presence.

He came down from heaven, published the good news of salvation, called and trained His disciples, breathed upon them the Holy Ghost, and went back to heaven without leaving behind Him any written Gospel at all. The legacy He left to the world was not an organized Church, nor a proud priesthood, nor a set of written documents, but the small band of disciples whom He had Himself prepared to carry on the work He came to start. In the fierce controversies of the present age it may help us to remember this. Christ lived and His salvation was proclaimed before any part of the New Testament was put into writing.

Men found rest and peace, and salvation in Jesus Christ, before there was a Christian Church, a Christian ministry, or Christian Scriptures. If the New Testament should suddenly be lost, and the organized Christian Church be destroyed, men would still find salvation; for the Spirit of God is in the world and moves upon the hearts of men and guides them into the way of peace.

THE APOSTLES', PREACHING.

On the day of Pentecost the disciples received their full equipment as witnesses for Jesus and preachers of the glad tidings of the Kingdom of God. Beginning at Jerusalem, they went forth to many lands to publish the good tidings of great joy which God had made known for all men. With their own lips, and not out of books, they told the story of their Lord's life; of His death; and His glorious resurrection and ascension into heaven. Out of their own experience and knowledge they spake the things concerning their Lord. They declared what they had seen, and heard and felt of the love of God.

Men believed the gospel which they heard. In many places they came together for worship and being of one heart and mind formed Christian churches for mutual help, long before the Gospels and Epistles were written.

What need had the disciples and their companions

of written documents at all? Had not they been the companions, the pupils, and friends of the Master? Three of them had seen His glory on the Mount of Transfiguration. Some were present when He called Lazarus from the grave. Many saw Him on the cross. Had they not also seen Him alive after His resurrection and witnessed His ascension to heaven?

THE APOSTLES LIVING WITNESSES.

The living witness was better than any written testimony. Writing could not describe the looks, the tenderness, the pathos, the sympathy, the patience, the mercy, the pity, and the deep love of our Lord, as could the witnesses which He Himself had chosen and fitted for this work.

But as time went on great changes came. The little company of the Apostles, the original witnesses, began to decrease. Some were killed, and others were growing old. So long as they remained, and could have access to the churches, all went well. But as Christianity spread, and the churches grew up far apart from each other, and the Apostolic band diminished, it was only natural that the converts should be anxious to have the precious words they had heard put into permanent form, so that they might hand them on to all who should follow them

A PERMANENT RECORD.

And the disciples themselves would be anxious to

have the story put into writing that it might endure. They came to know that the Gospel they had to preach was for all men of all time.

When the Holy Spirit led them to see this it naturally followed that they would desire the continuance of the story of their Master, which it had been the business of their life to tell.

These were, doubtless, the circumstances which led many, as Luke tells us, to take in hand to set forth in order a declaration of those things which were most surely believed among them, as those who were ministers of the Word, and eye-witnesses from the first, had declared them. Thus the Gospels sprang up.

THE WRITING OF THE EPISTLES.

Then, too, many of the churches which the Apostles had planted in different places called for special communications from their founders. Disturbances in some of the churches, unfaithfulness in others, the generosity of others, and the needs of many, caused the despatch of letters, all more or less embodying the teaching of Jesus, and containing statements concerning the mind and will of God, and filled with precepts and principles governing the duty of Christian men and women. All these writings were highly prized, and would doubtless be kept as treasures by the churches to which they were sent.

Though printing was then unknown, writing was common. It is quite likely that many copies of the Gospels were written at the request and at the expense of the various churches, while many of them would doubtless procure copies of the letters sent to the different churches. All these writings would be regarded as precious treasures by the various bodies which held them, and be deposited in safe keeping together with their copies of the Old Testament, and all considered and treated as sacred books. It is certain that at a very early period some churches had possessed themselves not only of copies of the Gospels, but also of most of the Apostolic Epistles.

It is the story of some of these precious documents that we have to tell, so that we may know from whence our New Testament came.

We shall have to go back step by step right to the fountain-head. We will begin by looking at three of the oldest Bibles in the world; then we will notice some of the ancient fathers of the church; then we will go back a generation and learn something of the Apostolic Fathers; and lastly, we will glance at some ancient versions of the Scriptures: we desire to see what they have to say to us as to our question—Where did our Bible come from?

III.

THE THREE OLDEST BIBLES IN THE WORLD

 WANT to take you now to see three of the oldest Bibles in the world. They are all written in Greek and are very ancient. The names by which they are known are "*The Alexandrian*" MS., "*The Vatican*" MS., and "*Sinaitic*" MS.

These three faded old books are very precious indeed, and are very carefully treasured by the nations who possess them. It is rather remarkable that they now belong to the three great branches of the Christian Church,—the Greek, the Roman Catholic, and the Protestant Churches. One of them, the Sinaitic (known as *Codex* Aleph) is in the library at St. Petersburg, and the Greek Church greatly prizes it.* Another, the Vatican (known as *Codex* B) is the valued treasure of the Roman Catholic Church and is in the Vatican library at Rome. And another the Alexandrian (known as *Codex* A) is in the British Museum, London, and is, of course, very greatly prized. I shall have a story to tell about

---

* Bought by the British Government in 1933 from the Soviet for $500,000.

each of these books when we go to inspect them; but I want first to state something about their age and how it is determined.

THE AGE OF THESE OLD MANUSCRIPTS.

It is not very easy to fix with certainty the exact date at which they were written. but we may feel sure that we are near the mark if we say they belong to the fourth and fifth centuries. If this be so, we may date them as from about the year 301 to 450 A. D.

But some readers may ask: How do we know the age of these manuscripts if they have no dates upon them? There are several ways of getting to know this, which I may explain in a few sentences. The form of the letters in which a manuscript is written; the way in which the words are joined together; and the plainness or ornamentation of the initial letters —*each* is a guide in fixing the date of a Greek document.

If you ever look at a Greek manuscript and find that all the writing is in capital letters and that the words in one line are all joined together without any division, you may conclude that it is of a very great age. It will be written thus, only in Greek charac-ters:—

GODSOLOVEDTHEWORLDTHATHEGAVEHISONLYBEGOTTEN
SONTHATWHOSOEVERBELIEVETHINHIMSHOULDNOTPERIS

The documents written in this way are called

uncial manuscripts, and are always ancient. Those which are modern are written in a running or flowing hand, and are called *cursive*. All these three old Bibles are uncial manuscripts.

If we could visit the British Museum we would see many copies of the Bible and other sacred books with most beautifully illuminated headings and initial letters. We would generally find that these are comparatively modern works. But the very ancient Greek manuscripts, of which there are many beside the three under notice, are usually very plain, and always in the *uncial* style.

I.—THE VATICAN MANUSCRIPT.

Come with me to the ancient city of Rome, that city which has played such a remarkable part in the religious and civil history of the world. If we have time it would be interesting while we are at Rome to visit the palace of the Caesars, and the house of Nero. We might see the Coliseum, the building into which Christians were flung to the wild beasts rather than part with their sacred books or dishonor their Lord and Savior. But we must go at once to the Vatican library.

The *Vatican* manuscript (*Codex B*) is kept here. This library was founded by Nicholas V. about A. D. 1448, and this MS. appears in the first catalogue, compiled in the year 1475. Nothing is known of its

CINETωNЄBΔOMHK
ςΓΤΑΒΑΣΙΑΕΓΟΝΤΟΣΚ
ΠΕΡΣωΝΕΤΟΥΣΠω
ΤΟΥΕΙΣΣΥΝΤΕΛΕΙΑΝ
ΗΜΑΤΟΣΚΥΕΝΣΤΟΜΑ
ΤΙΙΕΡΕΜΙΟΥΗΓΕΙΡΕΝ
ΚΣΤΟΠΝΕΥΜΑΚΥΙΟΥ
ΒΑΣΙΛΕωΣΠΕΡΣωΝΚΑΙ
ΕΚΗΡΥΞΕΝΟΛΗΤΗΒΑΙ
ΛΕΙΑΑΥΤΟΥΚΑΙΑΜΑΔΙΑ
ΓΡΑΠΤωΝΛΕΓωΝ ΤΑ
ΛΕΛΕΓΕΙΟΒΑΣΙΛΕΥΣΠΕΡ
ΣωΝΚΥΡΟΣΕΜΕΑΝΕΔΙ
ΞΕΝΒΑΣΙΛΕΑΤΗΣΟΙΚ
ΜΕΝΗΣΟΚΥΡΙΟΣΤΟΥΙ
ΛΑΗΛΚΕΟΥΨΙΣΤΟΣΚΑΙ
ΕΣΗΜΗΝΕΝΜΟΙΟΙΚΟ
ΛΟΜΗΣΑΙΑΥΤωΟΙΚΟΝ
ΕΝΙΕΡΟΥΣΑΛΗΜΤΗΕΝ
ΤΗΙΟΥΛΑΙΑΕΙΤΙΣΕΣΤΙ
ΟΥΝΥΜωΝΕΚΤΟΥΕΘΝ
ΚΥΤΟΥΕΣΤωΟΚΣΑΥΤΟ
ΜΕΤΑΥΤΟΥΚΑΙΑΝΑΒΑ
ΕΙΣΤΗΝΙΕΡΟΥΣΑΛΗΜ
ΤΗΝΕΝΤΗΙΟΥΛΑΙΑΔΙΚ
ΛΟΜΕΙΤωΤΟΝΟΙΚΟΝΤ
ΚΥΤΟΥΙΣΡΑΗΛΟΥΤΟΣ
ΟΚΣΟΚΑΤΑΣΚΗΝωΣΑ
ΕΝΙΕΡΟΥΣΑΛΗΜΟΣΟΙ
ΟΥΝΚΑΤΑΤΑΟΥΣΤΟΠΟ
ΔΙΚΟΥΣΙΝΒΟΗΘΕΙΤω
ΑΥΤωΟΙΕΝΤωΤΟΠω
ΑΥΤΟΥΕΝΧΡΥΣΙωΚΑΙ
ΕΝΑΡΓΥΡΙωΚΑΙΕΝΛω
ΣΕΣΙΜΕΘΙΠΠωΝΚΑΙ
ΚΤΗΝωΝΣΥΝΤΟΙΣΑΛ
ΛΟΙΣΤΟΙΣΚΑΤΕΥΧΑΣ
ΠΡΟΣΤΕΘΕΙΜΕΝΟΙΣΕΙ
ΤΟΙΕΡΟΝΤΟΥΚΥΤΟΣΝΙ
ΕΡΟΥΣΑΛΗΜΚΑΙΚΑΤΑΣΤ
ΣΑΝΤΕΣΟΙΑΡΧΙΦΥΛΟΙ
ΤωΝΠΑΤΡΙωΝΤΗΣΙΟΥΛ

CODEX VATICANUS.
(1 Esdras ii. 1-8)—Fourth century.
(Rome, Vatican Library.)

The Bible in Greek, written in uncial
letters, probably in the fourth century.
The text is arranged in three columns to
a page, except in the poetical books of
the Old Testament, which are written
in double column. Apparently in the
tenth century, the writing was carefully,
but quite unnecessarily, retraced in
darker ink. The same hand added the
breathings and accents. The MS. was
already in the Vatican Library in Rome
in the fifteenth century, but nothing is
known of its previous history.

previous history but
its present custodians
have guarded it with
the most jealous care,
and access to it was oft-
en difficult to obtain.
But thirty years ago,
Pius IX was the occu-
pant of Peter's chair,
and a photographic
fac simile was issued.

We notice that it
is in book form, hav-
ing more than 700
leaves about 12 in-
ches square. Each
page contains three
columns, except the
poetical books of the
Old Testament, which
are in double col-
umn; and the writ-
ing is all in capital
letters. It is almost
a complete copy of
the Bible. It has lost
Genesis, chapters i.
to xlvi., Psalms cv.

to cxxxvii., and all that follows Hebrews ix., 14.

THE OLDEST BIBLE KNOWN.

As we look at this book we may conclude that we gaze at the oldest Greek Bible known to the world. I say *known* to the world, because there may be other precious treasures older even than this hid away among the rubbish of some of the convents and other places, some day to be brought to light, as was the Sinaitic manuscript about which I am to tell you the story directly. But this is the oldest at present known. It carries us back probably to the beginning of the fourth century. For more than 1500 years this manuscript has been in the world; and it is a standing proof that if our Bible is an invention, it must have been forged before the fourth century, when this manuscript was written.

II.—THE SINAITIC MANUSCRIPT.

From Rome, in Italy, let us go to St. Petersburg in Russia. As we travel from the west to the east, from the center of the Latin to the headquarters of the Greek Church, I may say that we are going to see the famous *Sinaitic* manuscript (*Codex* Aleph).*

This is also in book form; each page contains four columns, except the poetical books of the Old Testament, which are arranged as in *Codex* B. It is believed to be almost, if not quite, as ancient as the Vatican

---

* Placed in the British Museum in London. Dec. 24, 1933.

ΚΑΙΔΟΘΗΤΩCΜΙΠ
ΜΑΚΑΙΗΛΟΙ ΡΗΕ
ΙΙΙΜΕΛΙΑΚΑΙΤΥΝΙΙ
ΗΑΝΑΡΕCΗ ΤΩΒΑΝ
ΛΕΙΒΑCΙΛΕΥCΕΙΑΝ
ΤΙΑCΤΙΝΚΑΙΗΡΕCΕ
ΤΩΒΑCΙΛΕΙΤΟΠΙΓΑ
ΓΜΑΚΑΙΕΠΟΙΗCΕ
ΟΥΤΩC
ΚΑΙΑΝΘΡΩΠΟCΗΝ
ΚΥΔΑΙΟCΕΝCΟΥ
CΩCΤΗ ΠΟΛΕΙΚΑΙ
ΟΝΟΜΑΑΥΤΩΜΑΝ
ΔΟΧΛΙΟCΟΤΟΥΙΝΙ
ΡΟΥΤΩCΕΜΕΕΙΟΥ·
ΙΩΥΚΕΙCΑΙΟΥΕΚ
CΦΥΑΗCΒΕΝΙΑΜΕΓ
ΟCΗΝΑΙΧΜΑΛΩ
ΤΟCΕΞΙΙΗΛΑΜ'ΗΝ
Η ΧΜΑΛΩΤΕΥCΕΝ
ΝΑΒΟΥΧΟΔΟΝΟ
CΟΡΒΑCΙΛΕΥCΒΑ
ΒΥΛΩΝΟCΚΑΙΗΝ
ΤΟΙΩΙΙΛΙCΟΡΕ
ΠΤΘΘΥΙ ΑΤΗΡΑΜΙ
ΝΑΔΑΡΑΔΕΛΦΟΥ
ΠΑΤΡΙCΑΥΤΟΥΚΑΙ
ΤΟΥΝΟΜΑΑΥΤΗC
ΕCΘΗΡ ΕΝΔΕΤΩ
ΜΕΤΑΛΛΑΞΑΙΑΥ
ΤΗCΤΟΥCΓΟΝΕΙC
ΕΠΕΛΕΥCΕΝΑΥΤΗΝΛΛ
ΕΑΥΤΩΕΙCΓΥΝΑΙ ΑΛΙΕ
ΚΑΚΑΙΗΝΤΟΚΟΡΑ
CΙΟΝΚΑΛΗΤΩΕΙΔΙΚΩΝΕ
ΚΑΙΟΤΕΗ ΚΟΥCΘΗ ΘΕΕ
ΤΟΤΟΥΒΑCΙΛΕΩC
ΠΡΟCΤΑΓΜΑCΥΝΗ
ΧΘΗCΑΝΤΗΝΠΟ
ΛΙ ΝΥΠΟΧΕΙΡΑΤΑΓ·

CODEX SINAITICUS.

(Esther ii. 3-8)—Fourth or Fifth
century.

(Leipzig. Royal Library.)

The Bible in Greek, written in
uncial letters, probably in the
fourth or fifth century. The text
is arranged in four columns to a
page, except in the poetical books
of the Old Testament, which are
written in double column.

MS. But its story is most remarkable. For generations, perhaps even for centuries, it lay beneath the books and rubbish of a convent, and was only discovered, as we say, by an accident.

There was a famous German scholar, named Dr. Tischendorf, who devoted nearly the whole of his life to searching for and studying ancient manuscripts of the Bible. All who love the Bible are placed under lasting obligations to him for his discoveries and investigations. It seems that he traveled through many parts of the East, searching all the old libraries into which he could obtain access.

MANUSCRIPT USED FOR LIGHTING FIRES.

In the year 1844 he was paying a visit to St.

Catherine's convent at the foot of Mt. Sinai, when he made a fortunate discovery. In the hall of the convent there stood a basket filled with parchments ready for the fire, and he was told two similar basketfuls had been burned.

On examining the contents of the basket he was surprised to find parchment leaves of the Greek Old Testament, the most ancient he had ever seen. He was unable to conceal his joy, and was allowed to take away one-third or about forty-three sheets. Though the lot was destined for the fire, his joy at his discovery roused the suspicions of the monks, and led them to think that perhaps the manuscripts were valuable, and so they would not give him any more. Tischendorf deposited the portion in the Royal Library, at Leipzig, to which he gave the name of " *Codex* Frederick Augustus " in acknowledgment of the patronage given to him by the King of Saxony.

SUCCESSFUL AT LAST.

But in the year 1859, or about fifteen years after his dip into the basket, he was again at the convent, armed with a commission from the Russian Emperor. His second visit promised to be a failure, and he was about to depart without having made any fresh discovery, but on the evening before he had arranged to leave, he was walking in the grounds with the steward of the convent, who asked him

into his cell to take some refreshment. As they conversed, the monk produced a bundle wrapped in
red cloth. To his great delight Tischendorf found
not only some of the fragments which he had
seen before, but other parts of the Old Testament,
and the New Testament complete, and some other
writings besides.

After a while, through the influence of the Emperor,
the manuscript was obtained from the convent and
brought to the Imperial Library at St. Petersburg, in
which we now see it, and it has become the most
precious treasure in the possession of the Greek
Church.[1]* A fac simile of this valuable manuscript is
to be seen in the British Museum.

If the contents of that one basket have so enriched
us, what a treasure we might have had if the contents
of those two other baskets had been saved from the
fire! What other priceless documents are yet to be
brought to light we cannot tell.

---

[1] See " *How we got our Bible*," by Dr. J. P. Smyth; and "*Smith's
Bible Dictionary*," for some of the suggestions of this chapter.

* The manuscript was purchased by the British Government in 1933
and is now in the British Museum in London.

IV.

THE THREE OLDEST BIBLES IN THE WORLD.—Continued.

III.—THE ALEXANDRIAN MANUSCRIPT.

ET us now return to England and visit the British Museum in London. Passing in at the main entrance and turning to the right we shall soon find ourselves in the Manuscript Room. There are many cases full of all sorts of ancient books, written on parchment of different kinds and ages. Quite a number of them are copies of the Bible. Some are lives of saints and others are on various subjects.

You cannot but notice the labor and skill and devotion with which many of them have been prepared. Pages of beautiful illustrations, numbers of elaborately decorated initials can be seen, looking as fresh as if recently done, though many of them are hundreds of years old.

ENGLAND'S MOST TREASURED MANUSCRIPT.

Our concern now, however, is not with any of these. We are going to see the *Alexandrian* Manuscript,—so called from having once formed part of

27

the library at Alexandria. This is the third oldest Bible in the world. It belongs to England, and is not likely to be lightly parted with. It is in four volumes, one of which you will find at the far end of the MS. room in a case marked F. If you speak to the Curator, he will tell you that large numbers of visitors come to see this famous old Bible.

You will notice that it also is the *uncial* form of letters, and has two columns on a page. In the same case will also be found photographs of one of the pages of each the Sinaitic and Vatican manuscripts. You will remember that the Vatican Bible has three columns on a page, and the Sinaitic Bible four columns on a page. This manuscript was probably written about the middle of the fifth century. It is written on very thin vellum, and has been in the possession of England since it was presented to King Charles I. in 1628 by Cyril, Patriarch of Constantinople.

It will thus be seen that it is the youngest of the three old Bibles we have noticed. It contains both the Old and New Testaments, though it is not quite perfect. It is marvelous to find a written document of such great age so perfect as this is. The New Testament seems to have suffered more than the Old. Only

TEN LEAVES ARE MISSING

from the Old Testament; but the new has lost more.

CODEX ALEXANDRINUS.

(St. Luke xii. 54-xiii. 4)—Fifth century.

(British Museum, Royal MS. r. D. v-viii.)

The Bible in Greek, written in uncial letters in the fifth century. The text is arranged in two columns to a page. It once belonged to the Patriarchal Chamber of Alexandria (whence its name), and was probably carried away by Cyril Lucar, Patriarch of Alexandria, who became Patriarch of Constantinople in 1621. Cyril sent it as a present to King Charles the First in 1628. It came into the possession of the British Museum with the rest of the Royal MSS.

Twenty-five leaves have gone from the Gospel by Matthew, two from the Gospel by John, and three from Corinthians.

We have now seen these three remarkable manuscripts all written, say 1500 years ago. It is not possible to estimate their value to Bible students. They carry us back at once to remote ages, and help very considerably in showing us where our Bible came from. As we look at them we are at once put in touch with men who lived at the beginning of the fourth century. Though in our study of ancient versions of the Scriptures we shall get much nearer to the Apostles and to our Lord than these three old Greek munuscripts carry us, we still have in them a rich boon. They link us with the Christian fathers of the early centuries, and clearly show that *their Scriptures and ours are the same.*

THESE MSS. INACCESSIBLE TO KING JAMES' TRANSLATORS.

It is quite worthy of note that the scholarly men who in the reign of King James made our Authorized English Bible, had no access to these three valuable old documents. The Vatican manuscript was at Rome, and the Pope of that day was not the man to let Protestants have the use of this book. The Sinaitic manuscript was buried in the convent at Sinai, and its existence was not known to the Company of Revisers. And the Alexandrian manuscript

was received in England about seventeen years after
the authorized revisers had done their work.   The
scholars who have prepared our excellent Revised
Bible were fortunate.   All these three old manuscripts were at their disposal.

CODEX EPHRAEM.

If this chapter is not already tedious let us examine at least one other ancient manuscript, which is in
the Library at Paris.   It is called the *Codex* of Ephraem.   It is believed to be nearly as old as the Alexandrian manuscript, if not a little older.   It was
brought from the East to Florence in the sixteenth
century, and in the middle of that same century
reached Paris.

At first sight it does not seem to be of much value, for its writing is in the *cursive* style and is
comparatively modern.   But as we will look at it a little more carefully we will see that under the modern

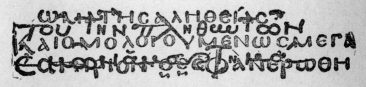

CODEX EPHRAEM (PORTION OF I. TIM., iii. 16).

writing there are traces of writing in the *uncial* or

ancient style. The parchment is doubly written upon. This kind of manuscript is called a Palimpsest, which means written twice. There are many documents of this kind. It would seem, in order to save cost of parchment, the writers would rub out as well as they could the first writing, and then use the sheets for writing other matter upon. It will at once be obvious that the ancient rubbed-out writing must in many cases have been far more valuable than the second or more modern writing. This was particularly so with the *Codex* of Ephraem, as the next few lines will show.

HOW THE OLDER WRITING WAS DECIPHERED.

The story of this precious manuscript is briefly this. It seems that about the twelfth century some one took this parchment and scraped and rubbed it to clear out the old writing, in order to make it fit for use again. When this was done the skins were used to write on them some discourses of Ephraem, a Syrian father of the fourth century, not one-thousandth part as valuable as the writing which had first been on the parchment. The old writing had not been completely rubbed out. Attention was drawn to it a long time ago, and efforts were made to read the faint writing. About sixty years ago chemicals were applied to the manuscript. The effect of this application was twofold; it much stained and spoiled

HEBREW MS.

(Exod. xx. 1-5)—Written earlier than A. D. 916.

(British Museum, Add. MS. 4445.)

Portions of the Pentateuch. The text is arranged in two columns to the page, and is accompanied by the Massorah Magna and Parva.

the vellum, but it revived a good part of the old uncial writings, and it was found to contain considerable portions of the Old Testament, and *fragments of each book of the New Testament.*

NUMEROUS OTHER MSS. IN EXISTENCE.

Though we have only examined four of these ancient manuscripts, there are large numbers of others beside. It is stated that in the *uncial* style there are 127 and in the *cursive* style 1,463. As time goes on greater attention will be paid to many of these, and no doubt we shall get much additional light upon the Bible as the result of their study. [1]

The conclusion to which we are brought by the ex

---

[1] See " Smith's Bible Dictionary."

amination of these old Bibles is, that our Bible was in existence when these books were written. Our New Testament, therefore, must have come from some *earlier* source. Let us take our next step.

THE ANCIENT FATHERS OF THE CHURCH.

ANY years ago, says Thomas Cooper, a party of scholarly men met at a dinner-party. During the conversation, some one in the party put a question which no one present was able to answer. The question was this:—

Suppose that the New Testament had been destroyed, and every copy of it lost by the end of the third century, could it have been collected together again from the writings of the Fathers of the second and third centuries?

The question startled the company; but all were silent. Two months afterwards one of the company called upon Sir David Dalrymple, who had been present at the dinner. Pointing to a table covered with books, Sir David said: "Look at those books. You remember the question about the New Testament and the Fathers? That question roused my curiosity, and as I possessed all the existing works of the Fathers of the second and third centuries, I commenced to search, and up to this time I have found the entire New Testament, except *eleven verses.*

It must be quite clear to every person that when these Ancient Fathers lived and wrote their books.

OUR NEW TESTAMENT WAS IN EXISTENCE,

or they could not have made such copious extracts from it as they did. Many of the books they wrote have been lost in the passing of the ages, and only a comparative few have reached us   But if the entire New Testament is to be found in such writings as have come down to us, we must conclude that the sacred Scriptures were not only known among them, but were their constant companion, their meat and drink, their precious treasure of the Word of Life— as is the case with us to-day.

In further illustration of this I may mention just one fact in connection with one of the ancient Fathers named Origen.   This man was a most active scholar, and occupied an important place in the Church.   He was born in the year 185, A. D.   He wrote many books, only a few of which have survived the ravages of time.   But we are told that in a few of his works which have come down to us, *two-thirds* of the New Testament can be found.   This is a most noteworthy fact.

It would make these chapters very long if I were to give some account of all the Fathers of the first three centuries which are known to us. I must leave those who desire fuller information to pursue their studies through the usual channels, and will content myself by selecting and naming only a few. Those whom I shall introduce will be men each of whom lived in the second and third centuries. Among them were some who lived when men were alive who had heard and seen the writers of our sacred books, and conversed with them about some of the august facts concerning our Lord's life and works, and some of them even the friends of the Apostles themselves.

THREE EARLY FATHERS.

In the year 175, three very eminent Fathers were alive. They are known as Irenæus, Tertullian, and Clement of Alexandria. I want to give you a very short account of each of these three; and it is important to note the valuable testimony which they bear to the existence, in their day, of the New Testament— *our* New Testament, observe. They lived in different parts of the world, moved among different circumstances, but all bear most valued testimony to the place and authority of the Gospels and Epistles in their day.

TERTULLIAN.

Tertullian was born at Carthage, in Africa, about the year 150, A. D. His father was a Roman centurion, and Tertullian was blessed with sound education in the religion of his heathen parents. Philosophy, history, and law were subjects in which he took much delight. He grew up to manhood before his conversion to Christianity, and was probably forty years of age before that important event took place. He was a man of profound mind, ardent and deep feeling, and a voluminous writer. This scholarly lawyer made great use of the New Testament. He ascribes the four Gospels to Matthew, Mark, Luke, and John. His works which are known to us have been carefully examined, and it is found that he makes 2,500 references to the New Testament. Of these 700 are references to the Gospels, and of these, again, 200 are to the Gospel by St. John. He quotes from every chapter in Matthew, Luke and John. He was the first to introduce the phrase "New Testament," and the first of the fathers who wrote in Latin.

IRENÆUS.

Irenæus was another type of man who lived in another part of the world and had entirely different surroundings. He was probably born in the year 130, A. D., and was a native of Asia Minor. He had the unspeakable advantage of being a disciple of Papias and Polycarp, the disciples and friends of the Apostle John. It is not quite clear how or when he came to leave his birthplace, but we know him chiefly for his connection with the Christian church at Lyons He was presbyter of the church there during the time of a fierce persecution under Marcus Aurelius the Roman Emperor. The aged bishop of the church, named Ponthinus, died in prison in the year 177, and Irenæus succeeded him.

In his writings he used the New Testament with great freedom indeed. He attributes the four Gospels to Matthew, Mark, Luke, and John. He argues that there were four and could be no more than four Gospels. In his known works he makes twelve hundred references to the New Testament. Of this number four hundred are to the Gospels; he makes eighty references to the Gospel of St. John alone.

CLEMENT OF ALEXANDRIA.

From Gaul we pass to Alexandria, that we may get a short notice of Clement, of that city. The early history of the church in Alexandria is not very certain. Tradition has said that Mark was the founder of it. Be that as it may, we know that Alexandria early became an important center—noted for its scholars, its library, and its university. It was the meeting-place of men of all nations. Christianity early took root in this city, and famous Christian schools were established.

Clement was probably born about the year 165, A. D. Like Tertullian, he grew to manhood before he became a Christian. He was a great scholar, and presided over a most famous school of thought at this center of active life and culture. He was a man of wide intelligence, and broad sympathies. Within one hundred years of the death of the Apostles of our Lord, he was working and teaching, and accepted as genuine and authentic the Gospels as we accept them. He mentions Matthew, Luke, Mark, and John by name, and places them in the order here last named. He makes three hundred and twenty references to the New Testament in his works which we have.

This is the testimony which these three ancient Fathers bear to our sacred Book. Living in different centres of life and thought, they yet all had our New Testament. They used it not simply as a private book, but as the recognized Scripture of the churches with which they each lived and worked. It must be quite clear that our Bible came from men who lived before they did; and as one of these men was a scholar at the feet of Polycarp, the disciple of St. John, we need but to go back one step more and we are with the Apostles. We want but one more link, and our chain of evidence, reaching from the Bible lying on my desk as I write, to the hands of the inspired men who wrote the New Testament portion of it, is complete. We will try to supply that one link in our next chapter, and thus clasp hands with the Apostles.

VI.

THE APOSTOLIC FATHERS.

ROM the Early Fathers we step back to the Apostolic Fathers. By the Apostolic Fathers I here mean men who were alive before the last of the apostles had passed away. They were the friends of the friends of our Lord; men who had heard the story of our Lord's life from the lips of His own disciples themselves, and from many of the intimate and close friends of these.

CLEMENT OF ROME, POLYCARP, AND PAPIAS.

Here again I select three: Clement of Rome, Polycarp, and Papias. In the last chapter we were considering the writings of about the year 175, A. D. Now let us go a hundred years farther back still, and fix in our minds the year 75, A. D. All these three men were born before this date. Polycarp may have been about five years of age, Papias perhaps fifteen years of age, and Clement a man, but of what age I am unable to say.

In this year, 75, A. D., it is important to remember that one of the Lord's disciples was still alive, and perhaps others. St. John was bishop of the church at Ephesus. His friend Andrew who went with him to Asia Minor, and also Philip who settled at Hierapolis, may also have been alive at this time. Jerusalem had been destroyed five years previously. The Apostle Paul had written his Epistles some years before this date on which we fix, and had now for some years been in the enjoyment of that "Crown of Life" which he tells us the Lord has laid up for the faithful in heaven. All the New Testament, with the exception of the later writings of John, was in the possession of the churches.

CLEMENT OF ROME.

When the Apostle Paul was a prisoner at Rome, he was very poor and in needy circumstances. One of the churches which he had planted—that at Philippi—made a collection for him, and sent it to him with good wishes and prayers. Their kindness to him at such a time touched his heart, and drew from him many kind words. He wrote them an affectionate letter which has been preserved and has a place in our New Testament as the Epistle to the Philippians. It stands among his many letters as one of the most tender, gentle, loving, and peaceful of them all. In the fourth chapter and the third verse he mentions a fellow-laborer whose name is Clement. John is thought by some to be identical with Clement of Rome.

We have no reliable history to inform us of the early life of Clement, just as we have but little to tell us of the early life of our Lord's disciples, and of the Lord Himself. In all probability he was a Jewish convert to Christianity, as were Paul and many of the leaders of the Christian Church in the first century. But though we know so little of his origin, we are not left in doubt as to his manhood and later life. He was an immediate disciple of the disciples of our Lord. He was the friend of several of them, knew them, was acquainted with their writings, and occupied a most important and influential position in the church.

POSSIBLY THE AUTHOR OF THE HEBREWS.

Many have thought that Clement was the author of the Epistle to the Hebrews, and some have said that he wrote the Acts of the Apostles. It is certain that many other works were ascribed to him; so great and influential was his place and name. He was third Bishop of Rome and such has been the respect in which his name and memory have been held, that almost a score of the Bishops or Popes of Rome have taken and used his name. At what exact date he died it is not easy to say. Eusebius, a learned man, who was born in the year 260, A. D., and died about the year 340, A. D., tells a little about Clement. This man, Eusebius, was the most famous of scholarly men in the church in his day. He wrote a history of the church from the Apostolic times to his own. In this chronicle he places the death of Clement in the year 95, A. D.

If this be correct, Clement was the Bishop of Rome at the same time that John was Bishop at Ephesus. How many of the disciples he knew we cannot say; but it is certain that he was the friend of several. He would thus be in a most favored position for knowing what was the teaching of the Apostles respecting our Lord's life and death, the account of which we have in our Gospels. And he would know of the other parts of the New Testament if they were then in existence. Have we any evidence that he did know of the New Testament? Let us see.

CLEMENT'S EPISTLE STILL EXISTS.

Clement wrote an Epistle to the Corinthians, which fortunately is preserved to us to this day. We have examined the precious old Bible called the Alexandrian Manuscript, the famous *Codex* A., which is in the British Museum, and which was written about the middle of the fifth century. Bound up with the New Testament volume of that priceless treasure is to be found with other inspired writings the Epistle to the Corinthians which Clement wrote. It has been translated into English and is now published together with the *Epistle of Barnabas and the Shepherd of Hermas.*

If you get it and read it through you will find that it is saturated with the language of the New Testament. In its doctrine, the style in which it is written, and its general thought, it is unquestionably based upon the New Testament. A copy of it lies before me and I have just been reading it again, and say without hesitation that it could never have been written by any man who did not know the New Testament as it was spoken and written by the disciples and Apostles of our Lord. It contains the words of Peter, James, John, and Luke. It has passages based upon the Epistles to the Romans, Corinthians, Thessalonians, Ephesians, Timothy, Titus, of James, of Peter, to the Hebrews, and the Acts of the Apostles.

Here, then, is another and most valuable link in the chain of evidence which shows that our New Testament came from the disciples and Apostles of our Lord. It confirms me in the faith that my New Testament is the same in substance which the church in the first century possessed. For if the disciples had not spoken and written the contents of the New Testament in those years of the first century, Clement could not possibly have written in their language. It is almost impossible to overestimate the importance of the writings of these ancient saints and fathers. The testimony which they bear to the existence of our Gospels and Epistles is such that, whether we believe them or disbelieve them, we are forced to admit that the Gospels and Epistles were in existence, or these Fathers could not have quoted them in the language in which they are written as they have done. This will be more apparent and convincing when we have added the testimony of Polycarp and Papias to that of Clement.

VII.

POLYCARP THE DISCIPLE OF JOHN.

POLYCARP'S name does not occur in the New Testament, but there are few of us who have not heard the story of his famous rejoinder to his persecutors. Brought before the Roman pro=Consul at Smyrna, he was given an opportunity of recanting while the fire was being prepared which was to consume his body. Urged by his judge, who was moved by Poly= carp's extreme age, to curse Christ and so spare his life, he nobly answered: "Eighty and six years have I served Him, and He never did me any wrong: how can I blaspheme my King and my Savior?"

Polycarp was born about the year 70, A. D. He had the advantage of Christian training, and was instructed in the Christian faith from childhood. He became Bishop of Smyrna. The Church at Smyrna was one of the seven named in the Book of Revelation, and of which it was foretold that "some should be cast into prison." He was put to death as a martyr about the year 156, A. D., being burned alive for his faithfulness to Jesus Christ.

Polycarp was a disciple of John, and was, some say, made bishop and set over the Church at Smyrna by the Apostle himself. If this be so, he must have early distinguished himself for his piety and devotion to religion.

Smyrna was not far from Ephesus. The Apostle Paul made a long stay at Ephesus, and only left it a few years before Polycarp was born. About the date of his birth the Apostle John and several other disciples settled in Asia Minor, John becoming the Bishop of the Church at Ephesus. Though Paul was dead at the birth of Polycarp, the memory of the great Apostle would linger long in the district of Ephesus among the churches which he planted, and with which he was so closely associated.

In Polycarp, then, we have another

MOST VALUABLE LINK IN OUR CHAIN.

If the books of the New Testament were in existence he would certainly have known of it. And if we find that he did know then we may accept his testimony as important and undeniable.

It seems that Polycarp wrote several Epistles to neighboring churches and some to private individuals; but with one exception all these have perished, and we now scarcely know their names. The one exception is a valuable letter which he sent to the church at Philippi, and which opens with th' following sentence:—" Polycarp and the presbyters that are with him, to the Church of God at Philippi: Mercy unto you, and peace, from God Almighty, and the Lord Jesus Christ, our Savior, be multiplied."

We are very thankful that this letter has escaped the ravages of time, and exists to-day as standing evidence that when Polycarp lived our New Testament was in existence, and was known to him. This letter of his shows clearly that the New Testament, even thus early, was so popular that it entered into the common life and language of the people. His letter to the Philippians is shaped in the language of our Scriptures, and it is evident even to a careless reader that it could not have been written at all except by a man who knew his New Testament.

It is a very short epistle, covering only a few pages, as it is printed in an English translation. Its length will be better understood when I say that I have read it through, timing myself, in ten minutes. Yet short as this epistle is, it is long enough for our purpose.

CHARACTER OF POLYCARP'S EPISTLE.

We learn from it that Polycarp was a devout and

pious man. We have already said that he had the advantage of Christian training, which was not lost upon him. From childhood he had listened to the great leaders and founders of the Church of Christ. He had sat at the feet of the saintly John, and from the lips of many who knew our Lord Himself; he had heard the story of our Lord's life, death, resurrection, and glorious ascension. He had heard them tell of the gift of the Holy Spirit on the Day of Pentecost, and of the rapid spread of Christ's teaching, and of the faithfulness of followers and their converts in times of trial and difficulty. All this had so filled his soul that he lived in close communion with God, and was deeply anxious for the welfare of the Church of God.

In his letter he urges the Philippians to be consistent in their conduct, steadfast in their faith, and to manifest brotherly love; while at the same time he warns them against falsehood, covetousness, and evil doing. Let us examine a few passages from this all-important letter.

"Wherefore girding up the loins of your mind, serve the Lord with fear, and in truth; laying aside all empty and vain speech, and the error of many, believing in Him that raised up our Lord Jesus Christ from the dead, and hath given Him glory. . . . But He that raised up Christ from the dead shall also raise up us in like manner, if we do His will, and walk according to His commandments, and love those things which He loved; abstaining from all unrighteousness, inordinate affection, and love of money; from evil speaking, false witness; not rendering evil for evil, or railing for railing, or striking for striking, or cursing for cursing; but remembering what the Lord has taught us, saying, 'Judge not, and ye shall not be judged; forgive, and ye shall be forgiven.'"

"Let us therefore serve Him in fear, and with all reverence, as both Himself has commanded, and as the Apostles who have preached the Gospel unto us, and the prophets who have foretold the Coming of our Lord have taught us; being zealous of what is good; abstaining from all offence and from false brethren, and from those who bear the name of Christ in hypocrisy, who deceive vain men. For whosoever does not confess that Jesus Christ is come in the flesh, he is Antichrist: and whoever does not confess his sufferings upon the cross is from the devil; and whosoever perverts the oracles of the Lord to his own lusts, and says that there shall neither be any resurrection nor judgment, he is the firstborn of Satan. Wherefore, leaving the vaunts of many, and their false doctrines, let us return to the word that was delivered to us from the beginning: 'Watching unto prayer,' and persevering in fasting: with supplication beseeching the all-seeing God 'not to lead us into temptation,' as the Lord hath said, 'The spirit truly is willing, but the flesh is weak.'"

PROOFS THAT THE GOSPELS WERE THEN WELL KNOWN.

These short quotations will be sufficient to show the nature of the whole Epistle, and also to show how it abounds with the language of the New Testament. In these few lines we notice—(1) He states the fact of our Lord's resurrection and ascension to glory. (2) He refers to the teaching of our Lord and His Apostles. (3) He refers to the *oracles* of our Lord, which was the word for the written Gospels. (4) He quotes the language of Peter, of Paul, of Matthew, and of John.

In the whole Epistle, which occupies but ten minutes to read, we find the language of Matthew, Luke, John, and the Acts of the Apostles; of the Epistle of Peter; and of Paul's Epistles to the Romans, Corinthians, Galatians, Thessalonians, Ephesians, Philippians, Colossians, Timothy, and Titus.

Here, then, we get a link in our chain which connects us to the actual writers of the New Testament, and assures us, beyond all possibility of doubt, that the contents of our New Testament were in the hands of the men who lived before the last of the Apostles were dead. Could anything be more decisive? Does not this most clearly answer the question, Where did our Bible come from? I do not know of anything ancient for which there is fuller and clearer evidence of authenticity than that our New Testament came from the disciples and their friends in that First Century of the Christian era. We can strengthen this last link still more by a short notice of Papias, another of the three fathers who was alive in the year 75, A. D.

VIII.

PAPIAS.

APIAS, like Polycarp, is not men-
tioned in the New Testament, but
he knew many of the men and the
friends of the men who are named
in it. In St. Paul's Epistle to the
Colossians (iv. 13,) you will find
that he mentions Hierapolis. This place, now in ruins,
lay only the short distance of a few miles from Laodicea,
and was about one hundred miles on the east of
Ephesus. A Christian Church was early planted
there, and the Apostle Philip is said to have settled
at that place.

Papias was the Bishop of Hierapolis. He was the
friend of Polycarp, from whom he received much
instruction; and some have said that he was a disciple
of the Apostle John. Papias wrote a work, called
"*Interpretation of the Sayings of the Lord.*" The
work seems to have been a large one; but, unfortunately, it is lost. Whether it has perished out of sight,
or is hid away among the dust and lumber of some
library or monastery, no one knows. The last trace of
the book seems to be about the year 1218, A. D. Fortunately, quotations from the work are preserved in the

writings of Irenæus and Eusebius; and though these
portions thus preserved are not nearly so numerous
as we would like, they are most valuable indeed.
We know how the Sinaitic MS. was discovered when
it had been thrown into a basket to be carried to the
fire. It is not many years since other precious
works of the early Christian times have been discovered; and if some day the work of Papias should
be found, it would add one more priceless treasure to
our ancient documents, and throw light upon our
New Testament.

HIS CAREFUL COLLECTING OF FACTS.

Papias was well acquainted with the daughters of
Philip, and would, doubtless, often hear from their
lips the story which their father had told them of the
chief events in the life of our Lord. It is said that
Andrew settled in Asia Minor with the Apostle John,
and that Papias knew both these Apostles; and many
of the intimate friends of the Apostles were known to
him. It will be interesting to look at a few lines from
his work, which Eusebius has preserved for us:—

"On any occasion when any person came [in my
way] who had been a follower of the Elders, I would
enquire about the discourses of the Elders—what was
said by Andrew, or by Peter, or by Philip, or by
Thomas or James, or by John or Matthew or any
other of the Lord's disciples, and what Aristian and

the Elder John, the disciples of the Lord, say. For I did not think that I could get so much profit from the contents of books as from the utterances of a living and abiding voice."

HIS EXCEPTIONAL OPPORTUNITIES.

If we look carefully at this passage we will see how important it is. It shows us at once in what a favored position Papias was in regard to ascertaining the facts of the history contained in our New Testament. Notice carefully the following which is known concerning him: 1. He knew two men who were disciples of the Lord. 2. He knew the daughters of the Apostle Philip. 3. He had met men who knew many of our Lord's disciples. 4. That he had conversation with them respecting the teaching of the disciples. 5. That he preserved "*books*" which contained these accounts. 6. That he added to the teaching of the books all he could learn from living men.[1]

It is very evident that any word which this man speaks on the question of the New Testament will possess the greatest value. His testimony will be second only in importance to the New Testament itself. A man occupying his position, and taking the trouble to get the true account of our Lord's work on

---

[1] Dr. Dale's "*Living Church and the Four Gospels.*"

earth, will be sure to leave a record worthy of attention.

He tells us that Mark was a companion of Peter, and that Mark wrote a Gospel. He also tells us that Matthew wrote a Gospel in Hebrew. He appears to have been acquainted with the Gospel of John, and he quotes from the early Epistle of John, and one of the Epistles of Peter. He knew the Book of Revelation, and maintained that it was a divinely-inspired book.

Though his testimony is not so full as that of Polycarp and Clement, it is only because we know less of him. If we had his whole work I have no doubt it would give greater testimony than either of the other Apostolic Fathers we have classed with him. He amply confirms what the others have said; and altogether they give such testimony as should make us all confident that our New Testament is not an invention but that it came direct from the Apostles of Jesus Christ.

I conclude this chapter, believing that it should make any person who reads it feel sure that his New Testament is not an invention. However unlettered a person may be who reads and loves his New Testament, he may continue to treasure and reverence it as the Word of Life, the Lamp of God, which has come to us from the holy Apostles themselves. Surely he may say, " I now know of a truth that this blessed Book has come down the ages, for I have seen that holy men in the Church of God have possessed it ever since the first century of the Christian era.   I know for myself, and shall be able to tell others ' where our Bible came from.' ''

IX.

ANCIENT VERSIONS OF THE
SCRIPTURES.

HE books of the New Testament were originally written in the Greek language. At a very early date some of these books were translated and copied into the languages spoken by the men and women converted to Christianity who did not know Greek.

The early versions of the Scriptures thus grew out of the necessities of the case. After our Lord's ascension to heaven, Christianity rapidly spread and took root in many lands. Within thirty years of the day of Pentecost there existed Christian churches, with their regular services and officers, in places far removed from each other. They were to be found in Europe and in Asia Minor, and Syria; also at Jerusalem, Cæsarea, Antioch, and in Rome. They existed in Asia Minor, and in the cities along the coast. Churches were found in Philippi, Thessalonica, and at Corinth.

Had the people in all these various places spoken the Greek language, their needs would have been met by multiplying copies of the original Greek books of the New Testament. But this was not so. It was necessary that the churches in these places should have records of the revelation which the Lord and His Apostles had made, in such language as they could understand. To meet their needs we know that translations were made. It is not easy to estimate the high value of these ancient versions of the Bible, bringing us back, as they do, to a date long before the oldest of our known manuscripts. They connect us with the Apostles, and form a most valuable chapter in the history of the Bible. If we can show that versions of the inspired books existed in the second century, we shall, of course, by that fact also show *that the Scriptures themselves were in existence before that time, or they could not have been translated into those languages.*

Out of the multitude of ancient versions I select two for special examination. These two versions are called *the Peshito*, used in the Syrian churches, and the *Old Latin* produced for the North African Christians. They were, so far as we know, the first versions of the Scriptures made. It is thought by some that parts of these two versions were made *within the Apostolic age*, and that shortly afterwards the translations of the separate parts were collected, and, after careful revision, were put together as completed books. Let us therefore examine the character of these two versions.

I. — THE PESHITO, OR SYRIAC VERSION.

The Peshito, or Syrian Bible, contains the oldest Christian version of the New Testament known to the world. The language in which it was written (the Syro-Chaldaic, or Aramaic) was the common dialect spoken in Pales-

SYRIAC MS.

(Exod. xiii. 14-16)—A. D. 464.

(British Museum, Add. MS. 14; 425,

Four books or the Pentateuch, viz: Genesis, Exodus, Numbers, and Deuteronomy, according to the Peshito version, in the Estrangela-Syriac character. Written in the city of Amid A.D. 464: the oldest *dated* Biblical manuscript in existence. From the monastery of St. Mary Deiyara in Nitrian Desert of Egypt,

tine at the time of our Lord, though Greek was much used in business.

It is quite impossible to fix the exact date of this ancient Syrian Bible. I venture to believe that *parts of it* were made in Apostolic times, and very likely under Apostolic direction. There is some evidence to show that messengers were sent from Edessa to Palestine to copy the sacred books, and that the Peshito version was made at a time before the last of the Apostles had passed away. We may take it as an admitted fact that the version *was completed in the second century*, and some time before the year 150, A. D.

This ancient Syrian Bible is a most important book. It was always regarded with respect, and in the earliest ages was received as an authoritative book. Indeed, we know that several other important versions were made from it into other languages— Arabic, Persian, and Armenian; and when the Syrian Church lost its unity, and split up into several opposing sects, all received this version as of authority, and all used it in their public worship.

These things all show it to have been of great importance. I venture the supposition that it may not only have been the most complete, but the most reliable collection of the sacred books then known to the world, except such as the church at Jerusalem may have possessed. The fact that it was probably a translation of many original manuscripts and careful copies of original manuscripts gave it an authority almost equal to the originals themselves.

It is important now that we should note the books which this version contains. It includes the four Gospels, the Acts of the Apostles, and fourteen Epistles of St. Paul, 1st John, 1st Peter, and James. You will see that this list very nearly corresponds with our own New Testament. It only omits the second and third Epistles of St. John, the second Epistle of St. Peter, the Epistle of St. Jude, and the Book of Revelation. It is very important to notice that, though this ancient version omits *five* books contained in our New Testament, it *does not include any book which is not to be found there.*

II.—THE OLD LATIN VERSION.

We have seen that the Peshito version was early made for the *Eastern* churches. We now turn to the Old Latin version, which was made for the Western churches, and which has exerted an influence upon them which can never be told by the pen of mortal man. It was from this version that St. Jerome made his Latin Vulgate, which Vulgate became the Bible authority of the Roman Church, and remains so to this day. And for more than a thousand years it was the chief source of nearly every version of the Scriptures made in the West.

But though we cannot fix the exact date of this old version, we are in possession of evidence which certainly carries us back to the second century. It was well known to Tertullian and men of his day. He freely uses it, and shows that it was not only known, but current at the time when he was in the midst of his literary activity.

Tertullian was born about 150 A. D. If we take that date as the year of his birth, and remember that the Old Latin version was in use in the African churches when he was a man and at work, it will not be unreasonable to suppose that it was written before the last quarter of the second century began. It may have been written much earlier, but it could scarcely have been much later.

The question now comes as to what books this Old Latin version contained. It contained the four Gospels, the Acts of the Apostles, thirteen Epistles of St. Paul, three Epistles of St. John, the First Epistle of St. Peter, the Epistle of St. Jude, and the Book of Revelation. It omits the Epistle to the Hebrews, the Epistle of St. James, and the Second Epistle of St. Peter. It will thus be seen that it contains all except three of the books which form our own New Testament.

If these two versions are put together, we shall get a more striking and important fact. We shall find that with the single exception of the Second Epistle

of Peter, which they both omit, *they contain all the books which constitute our New Testament, but no others.* Respecting these two versions, several things should be noted. *They were probably in common use by great bodies of Christians in the last half of the second century. The churches which used them received them as the heritage of a previous age. They represented the New Testament which was known, received, and revered, throughout the Christian Church, including both East and West.*

X.

OUR LORD'S BIBLE.

THE Bible which our Lord possessed was the Book we know and love as the Old Testament. Before His crucifixion there was not a single book of the New Testament in existence. The Bible which Jesus was taught to read as a child by that marvelous mother of His who knew the religious writings of her people, was the same old Book which our pious mothers teach their children to read in these days. The stories of Joseph and his coat of many colors, his slave and prison life in Egypt, and his exaltation to the place of command; of Samuel in the Tabernacle at Shiloh called up in the night by the voice of God; of David and his sling and stone with which he brought down the giant Goliath of Gath. These stories filled the young mind and heart of Jesus of Nazareth just as they interest boys of to-day all over the world wherever our Bible is known.

The fact that the books which form our Old Testament are the same which composed the Bible of the age in which Christ lived and died would be sufficient evidence to convince millions that it must have come from the inspired prophets of ancient days. For them it would be enough to know that it was read and honored and approved by their Divine Lord. If it had His sanction and that of His holy apostles, nothing else could be wanting. If it could be traced no farther back than the hands of Jesus Christ, His possession of it would furnish all the proof they would need.

THE BIBLE OUR LORD USED.

I shall, however, ask the reader to go with me much beyond the first of the Christian centuries; but we must take one step at a time, and make as sure as we can of our footing at each stride we take.

I want now to show that the Old Testament which we have was the Bible of our Lord and His Apostles.

"Ye search the Scriptures," said our Savior to the men of His time, "because ye think that in them ye have eternal life; and these are they which bear witness of me."[1] The Bereans are commended because "They searched the Scriptures daily."[2] Paul says that "All Scripture is given by inspiration of God."[3] St. Luke tells us that our Lord, "Beginning at Moses

---

[1] Revised Version, John v. 39. [2] Acts xvii. 11 [3] 2 Tim. iii. 16.

and all the prophets, expounded unto them in all the Scriptures the things concerning Himself."[1] And he tells us how the hearts of two disciples "Burned within them while He opened to them the Scriptures."[2]

The question at once arises, What Scriptures were they to which such frequent reference is made by our Lord and His Apostles? Did they mean the Old Testament we have, or some other?

WE HAVE THE SAME BOOK.

Any one who will take up a Reference Bible will very soon find out that Jesus, John, Luke, Mark, Paul, and the rest of the New Testament writers, had the same Old Testament which we prize. They are constantly referring to it and quoting from it. Let us see what use they made of it.

It would occupy too much space to mention all their quotations; and if we were to specify all their references, direct and indirect, we should find them to be very numerous. Each of the writers of the New Testament refers to the Old Testament, and they quote from most of its books. There are in the New Testament 190 references to the five books of Moses, 101 references to the book of Psalms: 104 references to the book of Isaiah; and 30 references to minor prophets. There are in the New Testament

---

[1] Luke xxiv. 27.   [2] Luke xxiv. 32.

some 639 references to the Old. These 639 references are spread over the entire New Testament, for all the Gospels and all but three of the Epistles contain quotations from or references to the Old Testament in some shape. In the four Gospels there are 191 references; 52 in the Acts; 67 in Romans; and so on.[1]

WE READ THE SAME TRUTHS.

It will at once be obvious that when we take up our Bible, and turn to read in the Old Testament portion of it, our eyes fall upon the same histories, prophecies, and poems that Christ's eyes rested upon.

When we hear passages read from Genesis, Isaiah, or the Psalms, we listen to the same truths which the Apostles and their Divine Master read and expounded in the ancient Jewish synagogues. We may with safety conclude that the Old Testament we have is the same which the Lord Himself used.

It matters but little to us that the original Hebrew manuscripts have perished. It will not in the least affect the object we have in view to say that the oldest existing Hebrew document does not date back more than a thousand years. We know beyond all possibility of doubt that nearly two thousand years ago the Old Testament was in existence. Our Lord could not have read it had it not been there. It

[1] For details see "*Angus' Bible Handbook,*" p. 333.

would have been impossible for Him to expound the Scriptures from Moses and the prophets, if Moses and the prophets had not been in His hands and accessible to His hearers

XI

THE PEOPLE'S BIBLE BEFORE CHRIST CAME.

ET us now go back to the ancient centuries to peep at people who lived three hundred years before Christ came on earth. It is a long way back; but we need not be alarmed for the Old Testament records events thousands of years earlier, and the last of its writers died before the time of which I am now writing. We want to know something about an old Bible which had a strange name, but which had a wide circulation, was very popular in many places, and in a wonderful way was blessed of God in preparing the nations for the Gospel of Jesus Christ, which was to be published when God had all things ready for it.

This book was called the *Septuagint*. It has a great deal to do with our Bible, and we cannot find out where ours really came from unless we know a little of this. This Septuagint Bible was in the Greek language, and was made from the Hebrew about the year 280, B. C. It was the first com-

plete translation of the Old Testament from the
original that was ever made that we know of, and was
certainly the most important.

I should like to tell if I could how it was made,
but unfortunately we have not much real history to
guide us.

ITS ORIGIN.

There are several pleasant stories which profess to
tell of its origin.   One of these says that the Egyp-
tian King, Ptolemy Philadelphus, was anxious to
have a translation of the Hebrew Bible, of which
he had heard much, that it might adorn the
great library which there was at Alexandria in the
third century before Christ.   The king's librarian,
Demetrius, told his majesty that he would never get
the translation of the Hebrew Scriptures so long as
he held so many Jews in slavery in his country.

The story goes on to say that the king set a vast
number of Jewish slaves free, and then sent valuable presents to the high priest, at Jerusalem, and
asked for scholars to be sent to him to make him a
Greek Bible.   The high priest and other officials
were greatly delighted, and selected six learned
men from each of the twelve tribes of Israel, and
sent off the seventy-two thus chosen to Alexandria
to do the work the king wished done.   For these
men he provided each a separate room, and they
began their work.   In seventy-two days each

is an immense congregation. On a pulpit of wood Ezra stands up to read the law of God to the newly returned exiles. Assisted by the chief men, he translates and expounds the Word of the Lord. Day after day this continues. The effect of this is that a few weeks later all the people confess their sins, and enter into a solemn promise to keep and observe the Law.

This is made all the more impressive by the fact that the priests, the Levites, and the chief men of the tribes solemnly sign their names on a parchment roll, and seal it as a sacred document to witness what they have done.[1]

THE "GREAT SYNAGOGUE."

The Jews tell us that the names on the list thus made formed the first members of the Great Synagogue. The chief work of the synagogue, which was a most important body, was to collect, select, and preserve to the world all the MSS. which compose the Hebrew Scriptures. Ezra was its first president; and at different times it had as members such men as Daniel, Haggai, Zechariah, Malachi, Zerubbabel, and Nehemiah. It is supposed to have ceased about the year 300. B. C.[2]

From the day when Ezra read the Hebrew Scriptures, and the solemn covenant was made by the

---

[1] See Nehemiah viii. x.

[2] Smith's "*Bible Dictionary*." Article, "Synagogue, the Great."

people, as reca ded in Nehemiah, to the day when the Septuagint was made, there is a space of time of only about one hundred and sixty years. The reading of the Law took place about 445, B. C. And the Septuagint was completed about 285, B. C. This is but a short interval. The two dates are sufficiently near for us to assume that the men who made the Greek version used the best known manuscripts; many of them, no doubt, the actual original documents bearing the signatures of their inspired authors.

THE JEALOUS CARE OF THE SACRED BOOKS.

We know how carefully and jealously the Hebrews guarded their sacred books. Josephus says: " During so many ages as have already passed, no one has been so bold as to either add anything to them or take anything from them, or to make any change in them; but it becomes natural to all Jews, immediately and from their very birth, to esteem those books to contain Divine doctrines and to persist in them, and if occasion be, willingly to die for them."[1]

We have now established the fact that the Septuagint was a Greek translation of the original Hebrew Bible—the messages which Moses, the Prophets, and the Psalmists, spoke to their fellow-countrymen, rendered in the Greek tongue. As our Old Testament contains the books of the Hebrew Scriptures, which

---

[1] *"Josephus against Apion,"* Book I. sec. 8.

ITS INFLUENCE.

The influence of this old Bible was marvelous, and the effect it produced in the world can never be told. It put the Scriptures into the hands of the people. It was the wide and far-reaching influence of this Book which prepared the world for the coming of the Great Prince, whose star the wise men who came to the cradle of the infant Christ had seen in the East. And it did more than anything else to prepare the Eastern world for the reception of Christianity. Our Bible came through this channel.

XII

THE FOUNTAIN-HEAD.

NE step more, and we are at the fountain-head. It is but a short journey from the Septuagint, the Bible of the LXX. (as it is often called) to the original source from whence flows the stream of Old Testament inspiration.

We have assumed that the date of the Greek version is the year 285, B. C., and that it was made by scholarly men from Hebrew manuscripts, and was the ~~~t ever so made.

~~ we can find out anything about their Hebrew manuscripts, and be sure they were there, we should know where the Old Testament portion of our Bible came from, for we shall be at the original sources. Let us see.

In the eighth chapter of the book of Nehemiah there is a marvelous description of the reading of the law which is worthy of careful attention. In a broad open space before one of the gates of Jerusalem there man had produced a translation, and when they compared them it was found that each copy exactly agreed with all the rest! This was taken to be an evidence that God had inspired them all. Not many believe the story now; but Josephus and many of the early Christian fathers not only told it, but doubtless believed it.

There is one thing about which we can be tolerably certain, and that is that the Septuagint, which had this name because of the seventy men engaged upon its translation, was made in the third century before Christ, and probably about the year 285, B. C.

Let me state, in few words, why I think it was made. It is well known to historians that when the Jews returned from captivity to their own land, they had almost forgotten the Hebrew language. This is not to be wondered at. Of those who came back only the smallest remnant had seen the land before. Two generations of them had been born in the land of captivity. In touch with the life of another nation and surrounded by influences that were powerful, it was no wonder that they ceased to speak the language of their forefathers.

Suppose a number of Welsh-speaking people, knowing only their own language, had been transplanted from their own country to the heart of the United States, and that they and their children remain there for seventy years—what would happen as to their language? In twenty=three years some of the children of these Welsh parents, born in the United States, would be married. In another twenty=three years more grandchildren would be married. A quarter of a century later the great= grandchildren would be married. Thus in about seventy years, all those who had come from Wales would either have died, or, if living, would be of a great age. Do you think these children, grand- children, and great=grandchildren would be still speak- ing Welsh? Their language would have dropped out of use. This was the case with the Jews. They had largely forgotten Hebrew.

But vast numbers of Jews never returned at all. When the last of the exiles reached home, about the year 445, B. C., they left behind them a larger number, known as the Jews of the Dispersion. The Septua- gint was made about one hundred and sixty years after the last company of Jews had returned to Palestine under Nehemiah. During that period the Jewish race had multiplied and spread enormously in those Eastern lands.

GREEK WAS THE COMMON TONGUE

of these Jews in many lands, and to meet their re- quirements and fulfil the purpose of God the Septua- gint or Greek translation of the Bible was made. It released the people from their dependence upon the priests for the Word of Life.

is an immense congregation. On a pulpit of wood Ezra stands up to read the law of God to the newly returned exiles. Assisted by the chief men, he translates and expounds the Word of the Lord. Day after day this continues. The effect of this is that a few weeks later all the people confess their sins, and enter into a solemn promise to keep and observe the Law.

This is made all the more impressive by the fact that the priests, the Levites, and the chief men of the tribes solemnly sign their names on a parchment roll, and seal it as a sacred document to witness what they have done.[1]

THE "GREAT SYNAGOGUE."

The Jews tell us that the names on the list thus made formed the first members of the Great Synagogue. The chief work of the synagogue, which was a most important body, was to collect, select, and preserve to the world all the MSS. which compose the Hebrew Scriptures. Ezra was its first president; and at different times it had as members such men as Daniel, Haggai, Zechariah, Malachi, Zerubbabel, and Nehemiah. It is supposed to have ceased about the year 300, B. C. [2]

From the day when Ezra read the Hebrew Scriptures, and the solemn covenant was made by the

---

[1] See Nehemiah viii. x.

[2] Smith's "*Bible Dictionary.*" Article, "Synagogue, the Great."

people, as recorded in Nehemiah, to the day when the Septuagint was made, there is a space of time of only about one hundred and sixty years. The reading of the Law took place about 445, B. C. And the Septuagint was completed about 285, B. C. This is but a short interval. The two dates are sufficiently near for us to assume that the men who made the Greek version used the best known manuscripts; many of them, no doubt, the actual original documents bearing the signatures of their inspired authors.

THE JEALOUS CARE OF THE SACRED BOOKS.

We know how carefully and jealously the Hebrews guarded their sacred books. Josephus says: " During so many ages as have already passed, no one has been so bold as to either add anything to them or take anything from them, or to make any change in them; but it becomes natural to all Jews, immediately and from their very birth, to esteem those books to contain Divine doctrines and to persist in them, and if occasion be, willingly to die for them." [1]

We have now established the fact that the Septuagint was a Greek translation of the original Hebrew Bible—the messages which Moses, the Prophets, and the Psalmists, spoke to their fellow-countrymen, rendered in the Greek tongue. As our Old Testament contains the books of the Hebrew Scriptures, which

---

[1] *"Josephus against Apion,"* Book I. sec. 8.

were translated into Greek for the Septuagint version, are we not safe in saying that the Old Testament portion of our precious Bible came from the men whom God in olden times inspired to tell forth His mind and will concerning the salvation of the world by Christ Jesus?

XIII.

THE FIRST VERSIONS.

E have now traced the Bible to its source. Step by step we have gone backward until we have reached the fountain from which came the water of life. Henceforth we shall always understand how to answer the question, "Where did the Bible come from?" We are now assured that the New Testament we have was possessed by the churches in the closing years of the first century. The Gospels which are in our hands to-day were in the hands of the Christian churches *before the last of the Apostles had passed away.* The Epistles which we possess as a sacred heritage and treasury of the highest Christian knowledge were in the hands of the bishops and officers of the churches eighteen hundred years ago.

The same words of hope, and love, and light which inspire and quicken us, came with all their force and power to the Apostolic Fathers. The story of our Lord's life and death, resurrection and ascension to heaven, which our Gospels unfold, is the same story which the Apostles related in the hearing of the men who put our Lord to death. It is the same story which two of the disciples and two of their friends and companions wrote in the four=fold picture of our Redeemer which the Gospels contain. All this should deepen our love for the New Testament.

And we are equally confident regarding the Old Testament. It is the sacred Scriptures of the Jewish nation and all converted to their faith and was possessed by our Lord and His Apostles. It is helpful to feel that when we teach our children the stories of the Patriarch, the sweet music of the Psalms, and the eloquent words of the Prophets, we are teaching them what Jewish parents taught their children in the time of our Lord. Nay, our Lord Himself was taught these same things when He was a child; and we see how the Scriptures entered into His very life.

ENGLISH TRANSLATIONS.

We have now another question to deal with, rather different from the one we have answered. The Old Testament was originally written in the Hebrew language, and the New Testament in the Greek language. To us these are strange and foreign tongues. They are languages which the masses of our people do not

know. But we have the Bible in English. *When
and how was it put into the English language?*

This is a most interesting question, and I will
answer it as well as I can. In answering the question
where the Bible came from, I have gone backward
step by step. But in answering the question of the
translation of the ancient Scriptures into the English
language, I shall adopt a different method. I shall
go back to the earliest information I can get, and
then work forward step by step to our own times.
A short history of our English Bible should not be
without interest for us.

FIRST TRANSLATED INTO LATIN.

St. John in his Gospel tells us that Pilate placed
on the cross of Jesus the words, "Jesus of Nazareth,
the King of the Jews"; and Luke says the same—
and that the words were in Hebrew, Greek, and
Latin. These three are the languages which have
had much to do with the sacred Scriptures. The Old
Testament was written in Hebrew, the New Testament in Greek; and by the middle of the second
century both Old and New Testaments were translated
into Latin. It was in Latin that we had the Scriptures at first; and, so far as we know, for many
centuries English-speaking people had to get the
story of the redemption from this language.

THE ENGLISH TRANSLATION A GROWTH.

I do not think any one can tell when the English

speaking people first had the Scriptures in their own tongue. It is quite certain that at a very early period the Latin Bible, known as the Latin Vulgate, was the Bible of the clergy and that used in public worship. It may have been that some portions of the Scriptures were translated into the common language of the people at a very early date; but it is doubtful if many were able to read them. Our English version is the growth of ages, and cannot be ascribed to any one man. The Old and the New Testaments in the original languages were the work of many men. God used a multitude of agencies, and sent us His revelations through a number of human channels In like manner, the production of the English Bible in its latest form, the Revised Version, has been secured by many men, working in different ways, each doing his share—God guiding the whole; until we have now what many hold to be the best English Bible the world has ever seen.

I cannot go through the history of all the translations; but will mention a few. I propose, first, to refer briefly to some of the early workers at our Bible; then to describe the work of Wycliffe, and of Tyndale, and a few others.

ST. JEROME AND HIS VULGATE.

If we should go to Bethlehem, and visit the church built over the spot where our Savior is said to have been born, the guide will take us to the Chapel and

Tomb of St. Jerome. About 383, A. D., Jerome, who was one of the most scholarly men of his times,

Helcceplusquamsplomonhic

ETCONDEMNABITEAD
QUIAUENITATINIBUS
TERRAEAUDIRE
SAPIENTIAMSALO
MONIS
CUMAUTEMINMUN
DUSSPSEXIERIT
ABHOMINE
AMBULATPERLOCAARIDA
QUAERENSREQUIEMET
NONINUENIT
TUNCDICIT
REUERTARINDOMUM
MEAM
UNDEEXIUI
ETUENIENSINUENITEAM
UACANTEM
SCOPISMUNDATAMET
ORNATAM
TUNCUADITERASSUMIT
SEPTEMALIOSSPS
SECUMNEQUIOR
ETINTRANTESHABITANT
ETFIUNTNOUISSIMA
HOMINISILLIUS

LATIN GOSPELS.

(St. Matt. xii. 42-45)— Sixth century.
(British Museum, Harley MS. 1775.)

The Four Gospels, in Latin, of the version of Saint Jerome, written in uncial letters in the sixth century.

went to Rome. The Bishop of Rome at that time was named Damasus, and he at once asked Jerome,

who had become his secretary, to undertake the task
of correcting and improving the Latin Bible then
used in the Western churches. He consented; and
in 385, A. D., he completed the revision of the New
Testament. After the death of Damasus, which oc
curred in the same year, Jerome retired to Bethlehem
where he founded a monastery, and where he lived for
thirty years engaged in useful works, pious devotions
and learned studies. It was here in the sixtieth year
of his age that he began a new translation into Latin
of the Old Testament from the Hebrew, a task which
not many men in his time were competent to perform.
He died at Bethlehem in September, 420, A. D.

His work was known as the Vulgate, and was the
only Bible which the English possessed for some centuries. For more than a thousand years it was the
Bible from which every version in English was made.
It is the Bible followed by the Roman Catholics in
all their translation work. What is called the Douay
Bible, with the Rhenish New Testament, was made
from the Vulgate.

XIV.

THE SCRIPTURES IN ANGLO-SAXON.

ET us imagine ourselves for a moment or two in a monastery at Jarrow-on-Tyne, on a quiet evening in May, 735, A. D. There, surrounded by his loving students, we might see an old man quietly dying. This was the venerable and beloved Bede, the most famous scholar of his day.

Bede undertook to translate the Gospel of St. John into the Anglo-Saxon, the language of the people of England at that time. Before his work was done, he fell sick and drew nigh unto death; but he would not relinquish his task. Calling his boy-pupil, Cuthbert, to his side, he bade him write while he dictated. It must have been a pathetic and touching sight to see him spending his last hours on earth in putting the writings of John into the common language of the people.

"There remains but one sentence, master!" said his pupil.

"Write quickly," said the dying man.

Soon the writer said, "It is finished, master."

"True, it is finished," said the dying saint.

He had been raised at his own request; and softly chanting, "Glory be to the Father, and to the Son. and to the Holy Ghost," his spirit took its flight and passed to the celestial city.

TRANSLATION BY A KING.

There were others before Bede who had done a little in translating some portions of the Bible.

Toward the close of the seventh century, metrical paraphrases of parts of the Bible were written by Cædmon, a servant at one of the Yorkshire Abbeys; and a little later Aldhalm, Bishop of Sherborne. translated fifty of the Psalms. This interesting work (the oldest of the many attempts to give the Bible in the vernacular of the English people) is still extant in a manuscript in the National Library, Paris.

We may now pass on to notice the work of King Alfred the Great.

Of all the kings who ever bore the title of Great, the Saxon king perhaps deserved it most; for he was a most remarkable man—a Christian, a scholar, a soldier, a statesman, and a king all in one.

Alfred was born at Wantage, in Berkshire, England. in the year 849, A. D. This was a little more than a century after the venerable Bede had passed away. Alfred had the advantage of a loving and pious mother. who not only trained him in the practice of virtue, but created in him a spirit of patriotism, and the love of learning. When he was a child of six years, he was taken by his father to Rome, and though so young, received impressions which were permanent. Amid the studies of his youth he obeyed the call to arms, fough⸗ the battles of his country, and began to reign when he was about twenty=two years of age.

Alfred was a man who practised strict discipline and great regularity in all things. His day of twenty= four hours was divided into three equal portions. He gave eight hours to business, eight hours to study and devotion, and eight hours to sleep and bodily exercise. In those days clocks and watches were not so common as now, so he invented a plan to measure his time accurately. He had candles of certain lengths and thicknesses made, which he consumed in lanterns, he knowing how long each would burn.

He took part in no less than fifty=six battles, and is said to have founded the English monarchy. He built England's first fleet of ships; established a militia; rebuilt many ruined cities, among them Lon- don; saved his people in time of war; ruled them wisely and well in times of peace; gave them wise, just, and humane laws; greatly encouraged commerce and manufactures; devoted a seventh of his entire revenue to public works; and founded schools and seats of learning. He died in the year 901, when but fifty=two years of age, after having reigned for thirty years. He concerns us now as a translator of the

Scriptures. He intensely loved his Bible, and was anxious that his people should be able to read it in their own language. Accordingly, he worked upon a translation of the Psalms, a portion of the Bible specially popular in all ages, and also upon the Gospels. His work was cut short by his somewhat early death; and, although we have no actual manuscript from his hand, doubtless his influence was felt in the subsequent Saxon translations.

THE WORK OF ÆLFRIC.

After the death of Alfred there came a long pause in Bible translation. Here and there, it is true, a little was done. Passing from King Alfred's work in the ninth century, we learn that at the close of the tenth, or early in the eleventh, the first seven books of the Old Testament were partly translated by an Archbishop of Canterbury named Ælfric.

In the early part of the fourteenth century there were two prose versions of the Psalms. But it does not appear that the whole Bible was ever known in the English language at an earlier date than the days of John Wycliffe, whose work we will notice in our next chapter.

XV.

JOHN WYCLIFFE

HE year 1382 is the earliest date at which it can with certainty be said that the entire Scriptures were known in the English language. This was chiefly the work of John Wycliffe, the "Morning Star of the Reformation," at whose life and work we must now rapidly glance.

Wycliffe lived in dark and trying times. The Church of God had sunk to a sad and desperate condition of spiritual decay. The lives of the clergy were a reproach to the name of religion. Men were promoted to a high position in the Church who were not only intellectually unfit, but who were scandalously impure in their conduct. The upper classes, too, were flagrantly wicked and unchaste.

REFORMER AND TRANSLATOR.

John Wycliffe was perhaps the first reformer in England who dared to stand alone and rebuke the leaders of the Church, and fearlessly assert the freedom of religious thought and teaching against the dogmas of the Pope.

It is with Wycliffe as a translator of the Bible that we have to deal. He labored hard to put the Word of God into the common language of the people, and succeeded to an extent which none before him had done.

THE FIRST COMPLETE ENGLISH BIBLE.

The whole of the New Testament, which was issued first, was the work of the Reformer himself, but in the translation of the first half of the Old Testament he was assisted by Nicholas de Hereford, one of his friends at Oxford. About 1382 he was able to send forth the whole Bible in the English tongue as generally spoken, and it was then that the *people* became possessed of that unspeakable treasure, the Word of God. The Bible was no longer merely the property of the priests and the few scholarly men of the time. It was now to be had in the mother-tongue of the people; and the dream of many—to enable every plowboy to read the Bible—was in a fair way of being realized. Wycliffe's Bible had a large circulation. But we must remember that it was in manuscript, for printing was not yet invented.

It is impossible fully to measure the influence which Wycliffe's Bible had upon the English people and upon the world. It was eagerly sought after by the people. Though it was sold at a high price, its treasure came down to the very poorest. Wycliffe's preachers went about the country reading the pages of the book, and telling of its contents in their sermons; and often parties were gathered together to hear some one read a page or two, or recite their contents.

This great work of Wycliffe laid all succeeding ages under deep obligation to him. As a translation it was not so perfect as the Bible which we now happily possess. We must recollect that it was but a translation of Jerome's Vulgate, that is, a translation of a translation. Men in those days had not access to the original manuscripts of which we have spoken.

WYCLIFFE'S PERSECUTION AND TRIAL.

Wycliffe's work was so well done that its influence remains upon our version to this day. Unfortunately, however, the men in office and power in the Church in Wycliffe's time did not appreciate the work of such a Reformer. Not only did he publish the Bible in the language of the people in 1382, but before doing this he had attacked the false and wicked position of the leaders in the Church; and for this attack he was called to account. He was summoned to appear before a great council at a monastery at Blackfriars, in May, 1382, with Courtenay, the Archbishop of Canterbury, presiding. There he stood alone—tall, pale, and thin. That brave man presented a great contrast to the dignitaries, clothed in their purple and satin and damask gowns, as he stood before his judge, surrounded by scowling abbots and monks, bishops and priests.

You may ask, For what offence is this poor, pale, friendless clergyman brought here? Has he been guilty of some grave crime? Does some nameless immorality sit upon his head? Has he been impure, unchaste, and wicked? Had such been his offence, he might easily have escaped. He had been guilty of a *serious* offence. He had attacked the Church, and denounced the sinful practices of some of her priests and monks. As did Luther at a later date, he spoke boldly against the sale of indulgences, and against masses for the souls of the dead, as systems of fraud and dishonesty.

Some consternation was caused during his trial by an earthquake which made London tremble. Many of the men in that assembly grew pale; but the arch-bishop declared that the trial must go on, and said that as the earthquake purged away the evil odors in the earth, so the trial would purge away the evil in the hearts of men which Wycliffe and his followers had introduced into the land.

The result of the trial was that after some days' consideration, a solemn condemnation was issued against the teaching of Wycliffe, and all who taught or received his doctrines. He returned to his home and his church at Lutterworth: and there during the last two years of his life, amid his books and poor parishioners, he translated and published the Bible as described above.

Doubtless much material had been gathered for this work during the earlier and busier portion of his life; but at Lutterworth he had the needful leisure for the completion of his life-work. He was assisted by his curate, John Purvey, in the work of revising and editing the whole; and transcribers then took in hand the task of multiplying copies, of which nearly one hundred and fifty were finished within forty years of Wycliffe's death.

The home-call of the Reformer was tragic in its swiftness. On the last Sunday of 1384 he was administering the Lord's Supper in his church. In that awful moment he fell to the floor, was seized with a fit of palsy and never recovered, lingering only to the last day of the year, when his soul passed on to that land where all is peace and love. But what a priceless legacy he left behind him!

XVI

WILLIAM TYNDALE.

ROM Wycliffe to Tyndale we take a stride of one hundred years. It is a long step to take, and it is a most important one. During that period a great discovery had been made, which was destined to play a great part, not only in the history of the Bible, but in the spread of knowledge all over the world: I mean the invention of printing. Wycliffe's Bible, and all books up to his time and after, were in writing. Monks in their cells and learned men in their studies toiled at the work of copying out the Bible with the pen. But when Tyndale was ready to issue the New Testament in English, he had the printing press to help him to multiply copies and spread them throughout England thick as autumn leaves.

THE PRINTING PRESS.

The printing press had at least a twofold effect upon the translation and spread of the Bible. Instead of men having to work for weary months at copying the Bible with the pen, its sheets could be struck off at a rapid rate. If the reader will sit down and *write* one page of the Bible, and mark how long it takes him, and then multiply the number of minutes which it occupies with the whole number of pages of the Bible, he will get some idea of the length of time taken to produce one copy of the Bible, without allowing any time at all for the initial letters and flourishes with which most of the Bibles were illustrated and adorned in the Middle Ages and afterwards. Let the same reader stand in a printing office and see with what rapidity the press throws off the sheets of the Bible.

Then, too, the printing press enables the Bible to be produced at a greatly reduced cost. In John Wycliffe's time Bibles were very costly indeed. There is a great difference in the purchasing power of money now and then; but it is estimated that in the fourteenth century a copy of the English Bible, as translated by Wycliffe, was worth a sum quite equal to $200 of American money. In our days a complete Bible can be had for twenty-five cents or less. This great invention of printing has been used to the full in the production and spread of the Scriptures. Every year millions of copies of the Scriptures, in whole or in part, are circulated in over three hundred languages and dialects.

It is almost impossible for us to understand and appreciate the effect produced upon the life of England by the rapid circulation and reading of Tyndale's Bible and those which immediately followed it. It was the one great book which England read. It did not take many years to make it the Bible of the people; and it, more than any other work, made English men and women the people of the Bible. It was read in all sorts of places, under all kinds of circumstances, and by all sorts of people. It rapidly found its way to the Universities. It was read by the merchants, the workers, and the plowboys. At the seats of learning, in the churches, and in the homes of the people, the music of that Book fell upon listening ears, and produced marvelous results. It kindled a remarkable enthusiasm among the people, quickened the moral sense of the country, and deepened the religious life of the nation. "The people who sat in darkness saw a great light."

TYNDALE AND HIS WORK.

But we must tell the story of Tyndale and his work. When William Tyndale was born, about the year 1484, John Wycliffe had been dead one hundred years and the great reformer, Martin Luther, was about one year old. The times were full of action and hope. The fifteenth century, in which he was born, and the sixteenth, in which he did his work, were centuries crowded with influences and forces which produced the great and powerful England of

to-day. Wycliffe and his Lollards had sown the seed
of the Reformation, which took root and was to bear
fruit during these centuries. It was the age of the
revival of learning—of patriots, of discoveries, mar-
tyrs, saints, and heroes. It was the era of able men
in many departments of life; and England saw a
great outburst of enthusiasm, which quickened its
social, intellectual, and religious life.

Not the least in importance stood William Tyndale,
the Gloucestershire boy. In early life he was sent to
Oxford, where he won distinction while quite young.
Afterwards he went to Cambridge, and came in con-
tact with those influences which pushed him on in
the great work of his life. Here he met with Erasmus
the foremost Greek scholar of the day, who published
the first Greek New Testament. Here, too, he became a Greek scholar, and was enabled to read and
translate from the original the New Testament which
he determined to publish in English.

He does not seem to have possessed much of this
world's wealth, so he sought the help and shelter of
the bishop of London, Dr. Tunstall. He was anxious to carry on his work of putting the Scriptures
into English under the roof of the episcopal palace,
and with the patronage of the bishop. One would
think that here he would be sure to find aid. But
unfortunately, he failed, so he betook himself elsewhere. Though he failed with the bishop, he succeeded with a London merchant of the name of Mon-

mouth, in whose house he worked for a considerable time.

DEPARTURE FROM ENGLAND.

He soon began to feel that he could not hope to be secure in London, or even in England, He saw many a man led off to prison, and some to death, for offences which would not be considered so serious as the work on which he was engaged. So in the year 1524 he left England to take up his quarters for a time at Hamburg. He never returned to England.

Here and at Cologne he toiled on bravely, amid poverty, disgrace, and danger, ever upborne by a brave heart and a hopeful spirit. At length his work was so far forward that the sheets of his New Testament were in the hands of the printer. But now, when success seemed within reach, a new and bewildering difficulty came upon him. An unprincipled and bigoted priest made some of the printers drunk, and got from them the secret of the printing of this book. He at once urged the magistrates to order Tyndale's arrest, and also send him across to England. Hearing of this through some friends, Tyndale rushed to the printers, seized the precious sheets of his book, and fled with all speed from Cologne to Worms.

Worms was then the stronghold of the Reformers, and was enthusiastic for Luther and his cause. Here, therefore, Tyndale found refuge. In 1526 he completed his book, and had copies ready for dispatch to England. But a new difficulty now faced him. How was he to get his book into the country? Though he had escaped from the mischief of the priests at Cologne, he knew that information had been sent to England about his work, and he was quite sure that a strict watch would be kept for it at the ports of entrance. In order to escape the vigilance of the watchers, the book was packed up in bales of cloth, in sacks of flour, and in cases of merchandise of all kinds. In spite of the care of the enemies of the Word of God, many hundreds of copies were thus introduced into England, and circulated far and wide among the people.

BURNING THE BIBLE.

While the lovers of the Book greatly rejoiced, its enemies were put into a commotion and panic. Finding it impossible to stop its entry into the country, the bishop of London hit upon the idea of buying up all the copies that could be found.

This was done, and the bishops had them piled in heaps and burned at Paul's Cross. The books blazed. But that did not stop the good work. The bishop could no more hinder the progress of God's truth than could the Nazarenes with their puny hands destroy Jesus Christ when they thrust Him out of the synagogue. Said Tyndale: "I am glad, for these two benefits shall come thereof: I shall get money to bring myself out of debt and the whole world will cry out against the burning of God's Word, and the overplus of the money that shall remain with me shall make me more anxious to correct the said New Testament, and so newly to imprint the same once again; and I trust the second will be much better than ever was the first.''

A fragment of the Gospel by Matthew is to be found in the British museum, the sole remaining relic of the original edition which was partly printed at Cologne. Of the second edition only two copies remain, so effectually did the enemies of the Word carry their plans into operation.

The work this man did produced lasting fruit. But, alas! the worker had only ill-treatment in return. He toiled on in exile, in poverty, and sickness for a few years. He worked away at translations of the Old Testament, but his career was cut short by the malice of his enemies and the treachery of false friends. Being some distance from his home one day, he was seized and hurried off to prison. Here, in a cold dungeon, he suffered much, until at last, in 1536, he was strangled at the stake and then burnt to ashes. He died with the prayer upon his lips, ''Lord, open the King of England's eyes.'' In his last hours his thoughts were of and for his enemies. How like Him who, when dying on the cross said, ''Father, forgive them, for they know not what they do.''

XVII.

AUTHORIZED VERSIONS.

HE blood of martyrs is the seed of the Church." In the case of Tyndale this was truly so, and the seed took root and produced a golden harvest. Though every effort was made to wipe out the work of the old Reformer who gave his life to translating the Bible into English, and printing and circulating it among the people, the work he did lived on after he was dead. In three years after he was killed, an authorized edition of the Bible in English was printed and circulated far and wide!

There was a law which said that all who read the Scriptures in the native tongue should forfeit land, cattle, life, goods—they and their heirs forever. They burned the books of William Tyndale, then they burned his bones; and many another brave man lost his life in housing and circulating the Bible. But in spite of all, Tyndale's work took root. It is not in the power of man to hinder the work of God. "Potentates have proclaimed their edicts, tyrants have lighted up their pyres, and mercenary legions have shed rivers of human blood to destroy the Bible and its believers''; but in spite of them all, it lives on. The more men have tried to eradicate the Bible the more deeply it has struck the roots; and the more they have tried to blot out the name of Christ, the more legible and glorious it has become.

THE BIBLE FOR THE PUBLIC.

William Tyndale was put to death in the year 1536. His offence was circulating the Word of God in the English tongue. It seems strange to us in these days, when the Bible is so much respected and loved, that men should have lost their lives in attempts to popularize and spread it among the people. Tyndale's death and the fate of the Bible shortly afterwards show us how God sometimes brings up one man to sow seed, the fruit of which others shall gather. Little did the men who burned his Bible and burned his body think that *in the space of three years* the Bible should be circulated far and wide, with due authorization.

THE GREAT BIBLE.

Such was the fact; for in the year 1539 an edition of the Scriptures, called "The Great Bible," was published under royal authority, and thus became the first authorized copy of the English Bible. From the year 1535, (one year before Tyndale's death), to 1539, several other editions of the English

Bible had appeared, which bore the names of *Cov‑erdale*, *Matthews*, and *Taverner*. These were for the most part based on the work of Tyndale, and the Authorized Bible itself was very little more than a revision of his work. Among the men who read the first national authorized edition of the English Scriptures at the king's command was Cuthbert Tunstall, bishop of Durham, who when bishop of London had refused to shelter and help Tyndale, and who had found the money to buy copies of the Bible for burning at Paul's Cross.

One almost wishes that the sturdy Reformer had been spared for a few years longer to witness the triumph of his work. It was his lot to labor while others enjoyed; to scatter what others should gather: and to sow what others should reap. In it all, how‑ever, God's Word was honored, the salvation of men furthered, and the glory of God secured.

After the publication of the first Authorized Bible, in 1539, the work of revision still went on. It did not —it could not—stop. Hitherto nearly all those who had worked at Bible translation had been compelled to carry on their work under great difficulties; some‑times in hiding, often an exile, occasionally in prison. No doubt the men who worked under these condi‑tions loved their work; but the circumstances did not allow them to produce such results as they would have done if they could have had free access to libra‑ries and other sources of information, and if they had been allowed that leisure and freedom which the best work requires. After the year at which we have arrived it was altogether different. Men could work at the Bible in open day.

THE ENGLISH BIBLE PUBLICLY HONORED.

It was only a little more than twenty years after Tyndale's death that Queen Elizabeth ascended the throne of England amid the universal rejoicings of the people. In her grand entry to the city of London she was presented with a copy of the English Bible which she pressed to her lips and to her heart as a precious treasure. Among the first acts of this Queen, we may note that she set at liberty all persons imprisoned for religion, and the exiles were allowed to return home to England.

Of the many editions of the Bible which appeared between the year 1539 and the year 1604, we need only name two.

The Geneva Bible was published in 1560. It bore this name because it was the work of many scholarly men who passed much time in exile at Geneva, which they devoted to this work. It was the most popular of all versions for more than half a century This was the first English Bible which laid aside the old black letter and appeared in Roman type, which divided the whole into verses, and entirely omitted the Apocrypha.

The Bishops' Bible appeared in 1568. This work

was undertaken by Archbishop Parker, who obtained
the assistance of a number of bishops. It was not a
success, and perhaps had less popularity than any
other English version.

THE AUTHORIZED OR KING JAMES' VERSION.

In less than fifty years from the accession of Elizabeth we find the king of England arranging for and
directing the great company of scholars who prepared
the splendid edition of the Bible which was to eclipse
all others and exist down to our day—the one honored
and treasured as the authorized version; than which
no book ever had a larger circulation, a wider influence, or a more glorious history.

In the early part of the year 1603 James the Sixth
of Scotland came to the throne of England as James
the First. He was a man of many indiscretions, but
was undoubtedly possessed of considerable scholarly
attainments. When he ascended the throne of England the three versions of the Bible which we have
previously noticed were in use. Six months after
his accession there was a conference on religious
questions at Hampton Court Palace, at which the
king presided. Here the question of a new revision
was mooted, and warmly taken up by the king.
He undertook the direction of the matter, and seems
really to have shown great skill and judgment in the
arrangements which he made and caused to be made.

THE COMPANY OF TRANSLATORS.

A company of fifty-four learned men were selected to carry out the work. They were chosen from many parties and schools of Englishmen, and included some of the best known scholars of the day. Instructions as to procedure were given to them, and rules formed for their guidance. After much labor and prayer their work was completed, and given to the world in 1611.

That they did their work well we may see in the fact that for more than two and a half centuries this version has remained in possession of the field. It is dear alike to the hearts of the rich and poor. It has found its way into the palace and the cottage. Its sweet and simple message is welcomed in the home of the prince and the peasant, and has been the light of life to countless thousands of souls.

XVIII.

THE REVISED VERSION.

HE Revised Version is considered by many to be the most correct English Bible the world has known. This will be easily understood by all if it is remembered how learning has progressed and what dis-coveries of valuable manuscripts have been made since King James' version was published in the early part of the seventeenth century, and that the result of all advance is embodied in our Revised Version.

It is no reflection upon the scholarly men who pro-duced the Authorized Version of 1611 to say that they were not so well able to give the sense of the ancient Scriptures as were the great company of mod-ern scholars who produced the Revised Version. Dur-ing the last two hundred and fifty years large numbers of men have devoted much time and attention to the study and comparison of the ancient manuscripts of the Bible. And to-day we are richer both in the number of eminent scholars and in the general knowl-edge of Hebrew and Greek than our fathers were. In 1611 the Sinaitic manuscript discovered by Tischendorf, as we have described in an earlier chapter, lay buried among the dust and rubbish of a monastery. The Alexandrian manuscript, now in the British Museum, was not in the country; and the Vatican manuscript, which lay in the library of Rome, was not available.

These three ancient manuscripts are among the most valuable in the world; but they were not accessible to the men who worked to produce the Bible which has held sway in England for so long. But all these, and many precious documents besides, were at the disposal of the men who have given us the Revised Version. It is thus seen that greatly improved knowledge of ancient languages, as well as the possession of more correct texts of the original Scriptures, have aided the men of these days in their great and important work.

WHY HAVE A REVISED VERSION?

Some have wondered why it was that any Revised Version was undertaken. The old book, they say, has served well for many generations; why could it not be left to go on its way?

We can quite understand this way of putting it; but if we think of the many and great changes which have gone on in our English language during the past two hundred and fifty years, we shall see that it was desirable to change many forms of expression in our version of the Scripture; forms which do not in some cases, convey correct meaning to the readers. And, besides, we know that in many places we did not get so near to the meanings of the inspired Word as it is now possible to get. Research in the languages used by the men who were inspired of God has yielded much information which was not within the reach of our fathers. All of these things and some others, not only rendered it desirable to have a fresh version, but enabled us to produce one better than that we had, good and excellent though it was.

THE REVISERS AND THEIR WORK.

It may be interesting to show in a few sentences how the revision was brought about, and how the revisers went to work. It was in the year 1870 that the decision was taken to get together a large and representative body of scholars who should be charged with the grave and solemn duty of revising the Bible. A company of able men, numbering some sixty-five, was appointed for carrying on the work in England. It is worthy of note that this company included scholars of all denominations. There were forty-one who belonged to the Church of England, and twenty-four belonging to other bodies, including, the Church of Ireland, the Church of Scotland, the Baptists, Congregationalists, Presbyterians, and Methodists.

In addition to this assembly, a committee of scholars was formed in America who should co-op-

erate with the revisers in England. This committee also included men of various denominations, and
numbered thirty-four. Putting both committees
together, we get the large number of ninety-nine
who took part in this holy and useful work. The
great company was divided into two committees: one
charged with the work of the Old Testament, and the
other with the work of the New. General principles
for the guidance of all were agreed upon. On June
22, 1870, the New Testament Company held its first
meeting; and on June 30, the Old Testament Company first assembled.

COMPLETION OF THE GREAT WORK.

We cannot follow these good men through all
their labors; but that they were diligent and faithful
is seen in the fact that the New Testament Company
alone held four hundred and seven meetings in the
years over which their work extended, and the total
number of attendances is reported as six thousand
four hundred and twenty-six. The Old Testament
Company did not reach the consummation of its toils
until June 20, 1884, thus having been at work
for fourteen years. The New Testament Company
finished its work, on November 11, 1880, and assembled together in a service of thanksgiving and
prayer to God for His goodness.

INTEREST IN THE NEW VERSION.

When it was known that the Revised New Testament was completed, the people eagerly looked for its publication. For the next few months printers and binders were hard at work upon the sacred volume, some thousands being employed. When the work was published in the following May (1881), it is said that one million copies were issued to the public during the first twenty-four hours; and in order to avoid the rush for the book, and to meet the demand for it as well as possible, the publication began at midnight. Not only was this New Testament circulated in all parts of the world, but nearly all the newspapers called attention to it by the criticisms which they made upon it.

America was as eager for the Word of God as England. Arrangements were made for its publication in New York on Friday, the same day on which it was issued in England. Chicago was as anxious to have the Bible as was New York; but as the fastest train then known could not travel the distance between the two cities in less than twenty-six hours, it seemed as if Chicago would have to be content to have the Revised Bible a day or two after New York had received it.

No train could reach Chicago on Saturday until after the stores and printing places had all closed. What was to be done? Were the inhabitants of this city to wait for the Scriptures until the following week? Not so, said the proprietor of one of the daily papers; Chicago shall have the New Testament at least within one day after New York gets it! Ninety telegraphic operators were set to work, and sent the whole of the precious Book, Matthew to Revelation, over the wires. Men were ready to set up the type in great haste, and the Revised New Testament was sold, complete, on the streets of Chicago on the next day after its publication in England and in New York.

It may well be doubted if anything so remarkable ever happened in connection with the sacred Scriptures either before or since. What would William Tyndale or John Wycliffe have thought about this great achievement had they been able to witness it?

NOTE:—When the work of revision was completed in 1885 by the English and American committees, as indicated in the previous pages, the members of the American committee pledged themselves not to sanction any other edition than that published in England during a period of fourteen years. They decided, however, not to disband, but to continue their organization and work in anticipation of a possible demand for a revision which should incorporate readings and renderings proposed by them and which the English revisers printed in an appendix, when not adopted in the text.

On the expiration of the fourteen years it seemed expedient that such an American edition should be issued, and this was accordingly done in the year 1901

The main differences between the English and American revisions are as follows:

The latter retains the name "JEHOVAH" in the text, instead of translating it as "LORD" or "GOD." It is more strictly uniform in the translation and use of other words It has modernized some expressions passed over by the English revision, and in many cases returns to the Authorized version's readings. It may perhaps therefore be said that the American revision is the best and latest result of Christian scholarship in giving a translation from the original languages into present-day English.

TEN REASONS WHY I BELIEVE THE BIBLE IS THE WORD OF GOD.

By R. A. TORREY.

 WAS brought up to believe that the Bible was the Word of God. In early life I accepted it as such upon the authority of my parents, and never gave the question any serious thought. But later in life my faith in the Bible was utterly shattered through the influence of the writings of a very celebrated, scholarly and brilliant sceptic. I found myself face to face with the question, *Why* do you believe the Bible is the Word of God?

I had no satisfactory answer. I determined to go to the bottom of this question. If satisfactory proof could not be found that the Bible was God's Word I would give the whole thing up, cost what it might. If satisfactory proof could be found that the Bible was God's Word I would take my stand upon it, cost what it might. I doubtless had many friends who could have answered the question satisfactorily, but I was unwilling to confide to them the struggle that was going on in my own heart; so I sought help from God and from books, and after much painful study and thought came out of the darkness of scepticism into the broad daylight of faith and certainty that the Bible from beginning to end is God's Word. The following pages are largely the outcome of that experience of conflict and final victory. I will give Ten Reasons why I believe the Bible is the Word of God.

FIRST, *on the ground of the testimony of Jesus Christ.*

Many people accept the authority of Christ who do not accept that of the Bible as a whole. We all must accept His authority. He is accredited to us by five Divine testimonies: by the testimony of the Divine life He lived; by the testimony of the Divine words He spoke; by the testimony of the Divine works He wrought; by the Divine attestation of the resurrection from the dead; and by the testimony of His Divine influence upon the history of mankind. But if we accept the authority of Christ we must accept the authority of the Bible as a whole. He testifies definitely and specifically to the Divine authorship of the whole Bible.

We find His testimony as to the Old Testament in Mark 7: 13. Here He calls the law of Moses the " Word of God." That, of course, covers only the first five books of the Old Testament, but in Luke 24: 27 we read, " And beginning at Moses and all the

prophets, He expounded unto them in *all the Scriptures* the things concerning Himself," and in the
forty-fourth verse He said, "All things must be
fulfilled which were written in the law of Moses
and in the prophets and the Psalms." The Jews,
divided the Old Testament into three parts — the
Law, the Prophets, and the Psalms—and Christ
takes up each of these parts and sets the stamp of His
authority upon it. In John 10: 35 Christ says, " The
Scripture cannot be broken," thereby teaching the
absolute accuracy and inviolability of the Old Testament. More specifically still, if possible, in Matt.
5: 18, Jesus says, "One jot or one tittle shall in no
wise pass from the law till all be fulfilled." A jot is
the smallest letter in the Hebrew alphabet—less than
half the size of any other letter, and a tittle is the
merest point of a consonant—less than the cross we
put on a " t,"—and Christ here declares that the Scripture is absolutely true, down to the smallest letter or
point of a letter. So if we accept the authority of
Christ we must accept the Divine authority of the
entire Old Testament.

Now, as to the New Testament. We find Christ's
endorsement of it in John 14: 26, "The Holy Ghost,
whom the Father will send in my name, He shall
teach you all things and bring all things to your
remembrance, whatsoever I have said unto you."
Here we see that not only was the teaching of the

Apostles to be fully inspired, but also their recollection of what Christ Himself taught. We are sometimes asked how we know that the Apostles correctly reported what Jesus said—"may they not have forgotten?" True, they might forget, but Christ Himself tells us that in the Gospels we have, not the Apostles' recollection of what He said, but the Holy Ghost's recollection, and the Spirit of God never forgets. In John 16: 13, 14, Christ said that the Holy Ghost should guide the Apostles into "all the truth," therefore in the New Testament teaching we have the whole sphere of God's truth. The teaching of the Apostles is more complete than that of Jesus Himself, for He says in John 16: 12, "I have yet many things to say unto you, but ye cannot bear them now. Howbeit, when He, the Spirit of truth is come, He shall guide you into *all the truth*." While His own teaching had been partial, because of their weakness, the teaching of the Apostles, under the promised Spirit, was to take in the whole sphere of God's truth.

So if we accept the authority of Christ we must accept that of the whole Bible, but we must, as already seen, accept Christ's authority.

SECOND, *on the ground of its fulfilled prophecies.*

There are two classes of prophecies in the Bible— first, the explicit, verbal prophecies, second, those of the types.

In the first we have the definite prophecies concerning the Jews, the heathen nations and the Messiah. Taking the prophecies regarding the Messiah as an illustration, look at Isaiah 53, Mic. 5: 2, Dan. 9:25-27. Many others might be mentioned, but these will serve as illustrations. In these prophecies, written hundreds of years before the Messiah came, we have the most explicit statements as to the manner and place of His birth, the manner of His reception by men, how His life would end, His resurrection and His victory succeeding His death. When made, these prophecies were exceedingly improbable, and seemingly impossible of fulfilment; but they were fulfilled to the very minutest detail of manner and place and time. How are we to account for it? Man could not have forseen these improbable events—they lay hundreds of years ahead—but God could, and it is God who speaks through these men.

But the prophecies of the types are more remarkable still. Everything in the Old Testament—history, institutions, ceremonies—is prophetical. The high-priesthood, the ordinary priesthood, the Levites, the prophets, priests and kings, are all prophecies. The tabernacle, the brazen altar, the laver, the golden candlestick, the table of shewbread, the veil, the altar of incense, the ark of the covenant, the very coverings of the tabernacle, are prophecies. In all these things, as we study them minutely and soberly in the light of the history of Jesus Christ and the church, we see, wrapped up in the ancient institutions ordained of God to meet an immediate purpose, prophecies of the death, atonement, and resurrection of Christ, the day of Pentecost, and the entire history of the church. We see the profoundest Christian doctrines of the New Testament clearly foreshadowed in these institutions of the Old Testament. The only way in which you can appreciate this is to get into the Book itself and study all about the sacrifices and feasts, etc., till you see the truths of the New Testament shining out in the Old. If, in studying some elementary form of life, I find a rudimentary organ, useless now, but by the process of development to become of use in that animal's descendant, I say, back of this rudimentary organ is God, who, in the earlier animal, is preparing for the life and necessities of the animal that is to come. So, going back to these preparations in the Bible for the truth that is to be clearly taught at a later day, there is only one scientific way to account for them, namely, He who knows and prepares for the end from the beginning is the author of that Book.

THIRD, *on the ground of the unity of the book.*

This is an old argument, but a very satisfactory

one The Bible consists of sixty-six books, written by more than thirty different men, extending in the period of its composition over more than fifteen hundred years; written in three different languages, in many different countries, and by men on every plane of social life, from the herdman and fisherman and cheap politician up to the king upon his throne; written under all sorts of circumstances; yet in all this wonderful conglomeration we find an absolute unity of thought.

A wonderful thing about it is that this unity does not lie on the surface. On the surface there is oftentimes apparent contradiction, and the unity only comes out after deep and protracted study.

More wonderful yet is the organic character of this unity, beginning in the first book and growing till you come to its culmination in the last book of the Bible. We have first the seed, then the plant, then the bud, then the blossom, then the ripened fruit.

Suppose a vast building were to be erected, the stones for which were brought from the quarries in Rutland, Vermont; Berea, Ohio; Kasota, Minnesota, and Middletown, Connecticut. Each stone was hewn into final shape in the quarry from which it was brought. These stones were of all varieties of shape and size, cubical, rectangular, cylindrical, etc., but when they were brought together every stone fitted into its place, and when put together there rose before you a temple absolutely perfect in every outline, with its domes, sidewalls, buttresses, arches, transepts— not a gap or a flaw anywhere. How would you account for it? You would say:

"Back of these individual workers in the quarries was the master-mind of the architect who planned it all, and gave to each individual worker his specifications for the work."

So in this marvelous temple of God's truth which we call the Bible, whose stones have been quarried at periods of time and in places so remote from one another, but where every smallest part fits each other part, we are forced to say that back of the human hands that wrought was the Master-mind that thought.

FOURTH, *on the ground of the immeasurable superiority of the teachings of the Bible to those of any other and all other books.*

It is quite fashionable in some quarters to compare the teachings of the Bible with the teachings of Zoroaster, and Buddha, and Confucius, and Epictetus, and Socrates, and Marcus Aurelius Antoninus, and a number of other heathen authors. The difference between the teachings of the Bible and those of these men is found in three points—

First, the Bible has in it nothing but truth, while all the others have truth mixed with error. It is true

Socrates taught how a philosopher ought to die; he also taught how a woman of the town ought to conduct her business. Jewels there are in the teachings of these men, but (as Joseph Cook once said) they are " jewels picked out of the mud."

Second, the Bible contains *all* truth. There is not a truth to be found anywhere on moral or spiritual subjects that you cannot find in substance within the covers of that old Book. I have often, when speaking upon this subject, asked anyone to bring me a single truth on moral or spiritual subjects, which, upon reflection, I could not find within the covers of this book, and no one has ever been able to do it. I have taken pains to compare some of the better teachings of infidels with those of the Bible. They indeed have jewels of thought, but they are, whether they knew it or not, stolen jewels, and stolen from the very book they ridicule.

The *third* point of superiority is this: the Bible contains more truth than all other books together. Get together from all literature of ancient and modern times all the beautiful thoughts you can; put away all the rubbish; put all these truths that you have culled from the literature of all ages into one book, and as the result, even then you will not have a book that will take the place of this one book.

This is not a large book. I hold in my hand a copy that I carry in my vest pocket, and yet in this one little book there is more of truth than in all the books which man has produced in all the ages of his history. How will you account for it? There is only one rational way. This is not man's book, but God's book.

FIFTH, *on the ground of the history of the book, its victory over attack.*

This book has always been hated. No sooner was it given to the world than it met the hatred of men, and they tried to stamp it out. Celsus tried it by the brilliancy of his genius, Porphyry by the depth of his philosophy; but they failed. Lucian directed against it the shafts of his ridicule, Diocletian the power of the Roman empire; but they failed. Edicts backed by all the power of the empire were issued that every Bible should be burned, and that everyone who had a Bible should be put to death. For eighteen centuries every engine of destruction that human science, philosophy, wit, reasoning or brutality could bring to bear against a book has been brought to bear against that book to stamp it out of the world, but it has a mightier hold on the world to-day than ever before.

If that were man's book it would have been annihilated and forgotten hundreds of years ago, but because there is in it "the hiding of God's power," though at times all the great men of the world have been against it, and only an obscure remnant for it, still it has fulfilled wonderfully the words of Christ, though not in the sense of the original prophecy, "Heaven and earth shall pass away, but my word shall not pass away."

SIXTH, *on the ground of the character of those who accept and of those who reject the book.*

Two things speak for the divinity of the Bible—the character of those who accept it, and, equally, the character of those who reject it. I do not mean by this that every man who professes to believe the book is better than every man that does not, but show me a man living an unselfish, devoted life, one who without reservation has surrendered himself to do the will of God, and I will show you a man who believes the Bible to be God's Word. On the other hand, show me a man who rejects the Divine authority of that book, and I will show you a man living a life of greed, or lust, or spiritual pride, or self will.

Suppose you have a book purporting to be by a certain author, and the people best acquainted with that author say it is his, and the people least acquainted with him say it is not; which will you believe? Now, the people best acquainted with God say the Bible is His book; those who are least acquainted with God say it is not. Which will you believe?

Furthermore, as men grow better they are more likely to accept the Bible, and as they grow worse they are more likely to reject it. We have all known

men who were both sinful and unbelieving, who by
forsaking their sin lost their unbelief.   Did any of us
ever know a man who was sinful and believing, who
by forsaking his sin lost his faith?   The nearer men
live to God the more confident they are that the Bible
is God's Word; the farther they get away from Him
the more confident they are that it is not.

Where is the stronghold of the Bible?   In the
pure, unselfish, happy home.   Where is the stronghold of infidelity?   The gambling hell, the drinking
saloon and the brothel.   If a man should walk into
a saloon and lay a Bible down upon the bar, and
order a drink, we should think there was a strange
incongruity in his actions, but if he should lay any
infidel writing upon the bar, and order a drink, we
would not feel that there was any incongruity.

SEVENTH, *on the ground of the influence of the
book.*

There is more power in that little book to save
men, and purify, gladden and beautify their lives,
than in all other literature put together—more power
to lift men up to God.   A stream never rises higher
than its source, and a book that has a power to lift
men up to God that no other book has, must have
come down from God in a way that no other book
has.

I have in mind as I write a man who was the

most complete victim of strong drink I ever knew; a man of marvelous intellectual gifts, but who had been stupefied and brutalized and demonized by the power of sin, and he was an infidel. At last the light of God shone into his darkened heart, and by the power of that book he has been transformed into one of the humblest, sweetest, noblest men I know to-day.

What other book would have done that? What other book has the power to elevate not only individuals but communities and nations that this book has?

EIGHTH, *on the ground of the inexhaustible depth of the book.*

Nothing has been added to it in eighteen hundred years, yet a man like Bunsen, or Neander, cannot exhaust it by the study of a lifetime. George Müller read it through more than one hundred times, and said it was fresher every time he read it. Could that be true of any other book?

But more wonderful than this—not only individual men but generations of men for eighteen hundred years have dug into it and given to the world thousands of volumes devoted to its exposition, and they have not reached the bottom of the quarry yet. A book that man produces man can exhaust, but all men together have not been able to get to the bottom of this book. How are you going to account for it? Only in this way—that in this book are hidden the infinite and inexhaustible treasures of the wisdom and knowledge of God.

A brilliant Unitarian writer, in trying to disprove the inspiration of the Bible, says: "How irreligious to charge an infinite God with having written His whole Word in so small a book." He does not see how his argument can be turned against himself. What a testimony it is to the divinity of this book that such infinite wisdom is stored away in so small a compass.

NINTH, *on the ground of the fact that as we grow in knowledge and holiness we grow toward the Bible.*

Every thoughtful person when he starts out to study the Bible finds many things with which he does not agree, but as he goes on studying and growing in likeness to God, the nearer he gets to God the nearer he gets to the Bible. The nearer and nearer we get to God's standpoint the less and less becomes the disagreement between us and the Bible. What is the inevitable mathematical conclusion? When we get where God is, we and the Bible will meet. In other words, the Bible was written from God's standpoint.

Suppose you are traveling through a forest under the conduct of an experienced and highly recommended guide. You come to a place where two roads diverge. The guide says the road to the left is the one to take, but your own judgment passing upon the facts before it sees clear evidence that the road to the right is the one to take. You turn and say to the guide,

"I know you have had large experience in this forest, and you have come to me highly recommended, but my own judgment tells me clearly that the road to the right is the one we should take, and I must follow my own judgment. I know my reason is not infallible, but it is the best guide I have."

But after you have followed that path for some distance you are obliged to stop, turn around and go back and take the path which the guide said was the right one.

After a while you come to another place where two roads diverge. Now the guide says the road to the right is the one to take, but your judgment clearly says the one to the left is the one to take, and again you follow your own judgment with the same result as before.

After you had this experience forty or fifty times, and found yourself wrong every time, I think you would have sense enough the next time to follow the guide.

That is just my experience with the Bible. I received it at first on the authority of others. Like almost all other young men, my confidence became shaken, and I came to the fork in the road more than forty times, and I followed my own reason, and in the outcome found myself wrong and the Bible right every time, and I trust that from this time on I shall have sense enough to follow the teachings of the Bible whatever my own judgment may say.

TENTH, *on the ground of the direct testimony of the Holy Spirit.*

We began with God and shall end with God. We began with the testimony of the second person of the Trinity, and shall close with that of the third person of the Trinity.

The Holy Spirit sets His seal in the soul of every believer to the Divine authority of the Bible. It is possible to get to a place where we need no argument to prove that the Bible is God's Word. Christ says, " My sheep know my voice," and God's children know His voice, and I know that the voice that speaks to me from the pages of that Book is the voice of my Father. You will sometimes meet a pious old lady, who tells you that she knows that the Bible is God's Word, and when you ask her for a reason for believing that it is God's Word she can give you none. She simply says:

" I know it is God's Word."

You say: " That is mere superstition."

Not at all. She is one of Christ's sheep, and recognizes her Shepherd's voice from every other voice.

She is one of God's children, and knows the voice which speaks to her from the Bible is the voice of God. She is above argument.

Everyone can have that testimony. John 7:17 (R. V.,) tells you how to get it. "If any man willeth to do His will, he shall know of the teaching, whether it be of God." Just surrender your will to the will of God, no matter where it carries you, and you will put yourself in such an attitude toward God that when you read this book you will recognize that the voice that speaks to you from it is the voice of the God to whom you have surrendered your will.

Some time ago, when I was speaking to our students upon how to deal with sceptics, there was in the audience a graduate of a British University who had fallen into utter scepticism. At the close of the lecture he came to me and said:

"I don't wish to be discourteous, sir, but my experience contradicts everything you have said."

I asked him if he had followed the course of action that I had suggested and not found light. He said that he had. Stepping into another room I had a pledge written out running somewhat as follows:

"I believe there is an absolute difference between right and wrong, and I hereby take my stand upon the right, to follow it wherever it carries me. I promise earnestly to endeavor to find out what the truth is, and if I ever find that Jesus Christ is the Son of God, I promise to accept Him as my Savior and confess Him before the world."

I handed the paper to the gentleman and asked him if he was willing to sign it. He answered, "Certainly," and did sign it. I said to him:

"You don't know there is not a God, and you don't know that God doesn't answer prayer. I know He does, but my knowledge cannot avail for you, but here is a possible clew to knowledge. Now you have promised to search earnestly for the truth, so you will follow this possible clue. I want you to offer a a prayer like this: 'Oh, God, if there be any God, and thou dost answer prayer, show me whether Jesus Christ is thy Son, and if you show me He is, I will accept Him as my Savior and confess Him before the world.'"

This he agreed to do. I further requested that he would take the Gospel of John and read in it every day, reading only a few verses at a time slowly and thoughtfully, every time before he read asking God to give him light. This he also agreed to do, but he finished by saying, "There is nothing in it." However, at the end of a short time, I met him again, and he said to me, "There is something in that." I replied, "I knew that." Then he went on to say it seemed just as if he had been caught up by the Niagara river and had been carried along, and that before long he would be a shouting Methodist.

A short time ago I met this gentleman again, and

he said to me that he could not understand how he had been so blind, how he had ever listened to the reasoning which he had; that it seemed to him utterly foolish now. I replied that the Bible would explain this to him, that the "natural man receiveth not the things of the Spirit of God," but that now he had put himself into the right attitude towards God and His truth, everything had been made plain. That man, who assured me that he was "a very peculiar man," and that methods that influenced others would not influence him, by putting himself into the right attitude towards God, got to a place where he received the direct testimony of the Holy Ghost that this Bible is God's Word; and any one else can do the same.